Immigration To Canada
Step by Step Guide

ISBN:
Publisher: Emjays Graphics
Rights Owner: Emjays Graphics
Copyright: © 2007 Standard Copyright License
Language: English
Country: United States
Edition: 2nd Edition
Pages: 184

Introduction

Canada Opens Borders to Immigrants

At times we all tend to contemplate our future prospects and we ponder about the life our family and loved ones will have in our home country.

If you are tired, poor, or part of the "huddled masses yearning to be free" you might want to set your sites on a shore about three hours north of where Lady Liberty and the famous golden door stand – Canada.

Canada is the largest country in geographic size in the western hemisphere with a population of only 31 million people. Its form of government can be characterized as a constitutional monarchy with a parliamentary democracy. It comprises of 10 provinces and 3 territories, with Toronto (4 Million); Montreal (3 Million) and Vancouver (2 Million) being the largest cities.

Canada is a young and dynamic country where immigration serves as the foundation for continued economic growth and which brings people, customs and traditions, rituals and culture to the forefront of current Government policy.

As Canadian permanent residents you and your family can share with Canadians and take part in the continued building of one of the world's most successful economic alliances involving Canada and the United States of America, its neighbor to the south. Indeed, Canada's esteemed stature is reflected in its being a member of the prestigious economic Group of Eight and its reputation as a respected participant in world affairs.

Canada is a land of opportunity and abounds with economic prosperity, sound and affordable education options, world renown health care and retirement schemes, an abundance of land, clean air and fresh water supplies, all providing for a safe and secure environment.

Embrace your future and bring the heritage of your past to a place where you and your family will be proud to refer to as home – Canada!

About Canada

Canada, also known as the "Land of Opportunities" has been assessed as one of the best countries in the world to live-in.

Some of the important facts about Canada are:

Canada's Landmass

Canada is the world's second-largest country (9 970 610 km^2), surpassed only by the Russian Federation.

Capital

Ottawa, in the province of Ontario.

Provinces and Territories

Canada has 10 provinces and 3 territories, each with its own capital city (in brackets): Alberta (Edmonton); British Columbia (Victoria); Prince Edward Island (Charlottetown); Manitoba (Winnipeg), New Brunswick (Fredericton); Nova Scotia (Halifax); Ontario (Toronto); Québec (Quebec City); Saskatchewan (Regina); Newfoundland and Labrador (St. John's); Northwest Territories (Yellowknife); Yukon Territory (Whitehorse) and Nunavut (Iqaluit).

Geography

Diversity is the keynote of Canada's geography, which includes fertile plains suitable for agriculture, vast mountain ranges, lakes and rivers. Wilderness forests give way to Arctic tundra in the Far North.

Climate

There are many climatic variations in this huge country, ranging from the permanently frozen icecaps north of the 70th parallel to the luxuriant vegetation of British Columbia's west coast. Canada's most populous regions, which lie in the country's south along the U.S. border, enjoy four distinct seasons. Here daytime summer temperatures can rise to 35ºC and higher, while lows of -25ºC are not uncommon in winter. More moderate temperatures are the norm in spring and fall.

Parks and Historic Sites

Canada maintains 38 national parks, which cover about 2% of the country's landmass. Banff, located on the eastern slopes of Alberta's Rocky Mountains, is the oldest (est. 1885); Tuktut Nogait, in the Northwest Territories, was established in 1996. There are 836 national historic sites, designated in honour of people, places and events that figure in the country's history. Canada also has over 1000 provincial parks and nearly 50 territorial parks.

Mountain Ranges

Canada's terrain incorporates a number of mountain ranges: the Torngats, Appalachians and Laurentians in the east; the Rocky, Coastal and Mackenzie ranges in the west; and Mount St. Elias and the Pelly Mountains in the north. At 6050 m, Mount Logan in the Yukon is Canada's tallest peak.

Lakes

There are some two million lakes in Canada, covering about 7.6% of the Canadian landmass. The main lakes, in order of the surface area located in Canada (many large lakes are traversed by the Canada-U.S. border), are Huron, Great Bear, Superior, Great Slave, Winnipeg, Erie and Ontario. The largest lake situated entirely in Canada is Great Bear Lake (31 326 km^2) in the Northwest Territories.

Rivers

The St. Lawrence (3058 km long) is Canada's most important river, providing a seaway for ships from the Great Lakes to the Atlantic Ocean. The longest Canadian river is the Mackenzie, which flows 4241 km through the Northwest Territories. Other large watercourses include the Yukon and the Columbia (parts of which flow through U.S. territory), the Nelson, the Churchill, and the Fraser--along with major tributaries such as the Saskatchewan, the Peace, the Ottawa, the Athabasca, and the Liard.

Time Zones

Canada has six time zones. The easternmost, in Newfoundland, is three hours and 30 minutes behind Greenwich Mean Time (GMT). The other time zones are the Atlantic, the Eastern, the Central, the Rocky Mountain and, farthest west, the Pacific, which is eight hours behind GMT.

Political System

Canada is a constitutional monarchy and a federal state with a democratic parliament. The Parliament of Canada, in Ottawa, consists of the House of Commons, whose members are elected, and the Senate, whose members are appointed. On average, members of Parliament are elected every four years.

Charter of Rights and Freedoms

Canada's constitution contains a *Charter of Rights and Freedoms*, which sets out certain fundamental freedoms and rights that neither Parliament nor any provincial legislature acting alone can change. These include equality rights, mobility rights, and legal rights, together with freedoms such as speech, association, and peaceful assembly.

National Emblem

The maple leaf has been associated with Canada for some time: in 1868, it figured in coats of arms granted to Ontario and Quebec; and in both world wars, it appeared on regimental badges. Since the 1965 introduction of the Canadian flag, the maple leaf has become the country's most important symbol.

The Canadian Flag

Several people participated in designing the Canadian flag. Jacques St. Cyr contributed the stylized maple leaf, George Bist the proportions, and Dr. Gunter Wyszechi the colouration. The final determination of all aspects of the new flag was made by a 15-member parliamentary committee, which is formally credited with the design. After lengthy debate, the new flag was adopted by Parliament. It officially became the national flag on February 15, 1965, now recognized as Canada's Flag Day.

National Anthem

O Canada was composed in 1880, with music by Calixa Lavallée and words by Judge Adolphe-Basile Routhier. In 1908, Robert Stanley Weir wrote the translation on which the present English lyric is based. On July 1, 1980, a century after being sung for the first time, *O Canada* was proclaimed the national anthem.

Currency

The Canadian dollar is divided into 100 cents.

Population

As of the summer of 1996, Canada's population was over 30 million.

Main Cities

As of July 1, 1996, the leading Canadian cities are Toronto (4.44 million), Montreal (3.36 million), Vancouver (1.89 million), Ottawa-Hull, the National Capital Region (1.03 million).

Distribution of Population

A large majority of Canadians, 77 percent, live in cities and towns.

Family Size

At the time of the 1996 national census, the average family size was 3.1, including 1.2 children.

Living Standard

Canada ranks sixth in the world in standard of living (measured according to gross domestic product per capita), behind only the United States, Switzerland, Luxembourg, Germany, and Japan. Canada's rank among nations tends to rise even higher in assessments that consider GDP per capita along with other factors (e.g., life expectancy, education) that contribute to "quality of life."

Health Care and Social Security

Basic health care, with the exception of dental services, is free at the point of delivery. And prescription drugs are in most cases dispensed without charge to people over 65 and social aid recipients. Canada also has an extensive social security network, including an old age pension, a family allowance, unemployment insurance and welfare.

Aboriginal Peoples

In 1996, about 3% of Canadians belonged to one or more of the three Aboriginal groups recognized by the Constitution Act, 1982: North American Indian, Métis, or Inuit. Of this percentage, about 69% are North American Indian, 26% Métis, and 5% Inuit.

Religion

According to the 1991 census, more than four-fifths of Canadians are Christian, with Catholics accounting for about 47% of the population and Protestants about 36%. Other religions include Judaism, Islam, Hinduism, Sikhism and Buddhism. Some 12.5%, more than any single denomination except Roman Catholic, have no religious affiliation at all.

Languages

Canada has two official languages: English, the mother tongue of about 59% of Canadians; and French, the first language of 23% of the population. A full 18% have either more than one mother tongue or a mother tongue other than English or French, such as Chinese, Italian, German, Polish, Spanish, Portuguese, Punjabi, Ukrainian, Arabic, Dutch, Tagalog, Greek, Vietnamese, Cree, Inuktitut, or other languages.

The *Official Languages Act* makes French and English the official languages of Canada and provides for special measures aimed at enhancing the vitality and supporting the development of English and French linguistic minority communities. Canada's federal institutions reflect the equality of its two official languages by offering bilingual services.

Ethnic Origin

In 1996, about 19% of the population reported "Canadian" as their single ethnic origin, with 17% reporting British Isles-only ancestry and 9% French-only ancestry. About 10% reported a combination of British Isles, French, or Canadian origin, with another 16% reporting an ancestry of either British Isles, French or Canadian in combination with some other origin. Some 28% reported origins other than the British Isles, French or Canadian.

Education

The educational system varies from province to province and includes six to eight years of elementary school, four or five years of secondary school and three or four years at the university undergraduate level. The 1996 census revealed that, among Canadians aged 15 and over, about 23% had graduated from secondary school, some 9% had bachelor's degrees, and about 6% had advanced degrees.

Sports

Canada's most popular sports include swimming, ice hockey, cross-country and alpine skiing, baseball, tennis, basketball and golf. Ice hockey and lacrosse are Canada's national sports.

Main Natural Resources

The principal natural resources are natural gas, oil, gold, coal, copper, iron ore, nickel, potash, uranium and zinc, along with wood and water.

Leading Industries

These include automobile manufacturing, pulp and paper, iron and steel work, machinery and equipment manufacturing, mining, extraction of fossil fuels, forestry and agriculture.

Exports

Canada's leading exports are automobile vehicles and parts, machinery and equipment, high-technology products, oil, natural gas, metals, and forest and farm products.

Immigrating to Canada

Every year, Canada welcomes thousands of new residents. Coming to Canada as an immigrant is an exciting opportunity, but also a great challenge.

If you are interested in immigrating to Canada, you have a number of options when applying for permanent residence status. Read about these programs and decide which class suits you and your family best.

Skilled Worker Class Immigration:
Canada values the skills and experiences that foreign professionals and workers bring with them. Check to see if your skills and experience qualify you to come to Canada as a skilled worker.

Business Class Immigration:
Canada has a strong economic culture. If you have experience running or investing in businesses, you may qualify to come to Canada as a business immigrant.

Provincial Nomination:
Most Canadian provinces have programs that encourage immigrants to settle in those provinces and benefit their economies. Learn about settling in one of Canada's provinces as a provincial nominee.

Family Class Immigration:
Family class immigration reunites families in Canadian homes. Learn how to sponsor your family member or come to Canada as a member of the family class.

International Adoption:
Adopting children from abroad can be a long process. This is to protect children's rights. Learn about what you need to do to bring an adoptive child to Canada.

Quebec-Selected Immigration:
Quebec is responsible for selecting immigrants who wish to settle in Quebec. Find out how to apply to be selected to settle in Quebec.

Skilled Worker Class

Skilled workers and professionals

Skilled workers have education, work experience, knowledge of English or French, and other abilities that will help them to establish themselves successfully as permanent residents in Canada.

Making an application to immigrate to Canada is straightforward. This section will help you to find guides, information and the forms you need to make your application.

The rules for applying as a skilled worker can change from time to time, so make sure you visit this site regularly if you are considering immigrating to Canada as a skilled worker.

Before you apply, make sure you refer to updated selection criteria, and are familiar with the current application procedures. After you apply, make sure you return to this web page to find out about the steps that follow.

Note: You must meet the following minimum requirements to apply as a skilled worker:

- You have at least one continuous year of full-time, paid work experience or the equivalent in part-time continuous employment.

- Your work experience must be Skill Type 0 (managerial occupations) or Skill Level A (professional occupations) or B (technical occupations and skilled trades) on the Canadian National Occupational Classification (NOC).

- You must have had this experience within the last 10 years.

Definition:

Skilled workers are people who may become permanent residents based on their ability to become economically established in Canada.

Minimum requirement

For your application to be considered, you must meet the minimum requirement of at least one year of full-time (or full-time equivalent), paid work experience. This experience must:

- have occurred in the past 10 years

- be in Skill Type 0 or Skill Level A or B of the National Occupation Classification (NOC).

The National Occupation Classification (NOC)

The NOC is a classification system of occupations in Canada. It describes the duties, skills, aptitudes and work settings typical of jobs in the Canadian labour market.

Determining your NOC category

Follow these steps to determine if your work experience is in an occupation that meets the minimum requirement to apply as a skilled worker:

STEP 1. Go to page Occupational List and Point Grid in this Book

STEP 2. See if your work experience qualifies you to immigrate under the Skilled Worker class.

STEP 3. If you have experience in more than one occupation during the past 10 years, repeat the search to determine if you meet the minimum requirement to apply as a skilled worker. Work experience in several occupations may also be used, if it adds up to one full year.

STEP 4. Check the list of restricted occupations. If your work experience is in a restricted occupation, then it **cannot** be used to earn points to qualify for the skilled worker class. (At the time of printing there were no restricted occupations in Canada; however, you should check our Web site to see the current list.)

You are not eligible to apply as a skilled worker if:

- none of your work experience is listed in Skill Type 0 or Skill Level A or B of the NOC;

- your experience did not occur within 10 years of the date of application

- your eligible work experience does not add up to one full year; or

- your only work experience is in a restricted occupation.

Selection system

If your work experience meets the minimum requirements to apply as a skilled worker, your application will be assessed against two criteria:

1. Required funds

2. Selection factors

Disclosure of funds

You will have to tell a Canadian official if you carry more than $10,000 Canadian in cash funds upon your entry to Canada. This could be in the form of:

- money (coins or bank notes)

- securities in bearer form (stocks, bonds, debentures, treasury bills etc.)

- negotiable instruments in bearer form (bankers' drafts, cheques, travellers' cheques, money orders etc.)

Failure to disclose can result in fines and imprisonment.

How to estimate your points

Read the explanation for each factor, then fill in your score on the worksheet.

If you have a spouse or common-law partner, you must decide which of you will be the principal applicant; the other person will be considered a family member. Use the self-assessment worksheet to determine which of you would score the most points. This person should be the principal applicant.

> **Note: A common-law partner** is a person of the same or opposite sex who has lived with you in a conjugal relationship for a period of at least one year.

> **A family member** is a spouse, common-law partner or dependent child included in your application.

FACTOR 1: EDUCATION (MAXIMUM 25 POINTS)

Points are awarded for earned educational credentials as well as the number of years of full-time or full-time equivalent study. To be awarded points, you must meet **both** stated criteria. See page: Point Grid in this Chapter for details.

> **Note: Full-time studies:** At least 15 hours of instruction per week during the academic year. This includes any period of workplace training that forms part of the course.

> **Full-time equivalent studies:** If you completed a program of study on a part-time or accelerated basis, count the length of time it would have taken to complete the program on a full-time basis.

Instructions

If you have not completed the number of years of study that correspond to your highest educational credential, award yourself points based on the number of years of study.

> **Examples:** If you have a Master's degree but have completed only 16 years of full-time study, award yourself 22 points. If you have a four-year Bachelor's degree and have completed 14 or more years of study, award yourself 20 points.

FACTOR 2: LANGUAGE ABILITY (MAXIMUM 24 POINTS)

Points are awarded for proven ability in reading, writing, listening to and speaking English and/or French. See page: Language Proficincy Tests for details.

Instructions

STEP 1. If you have some abilities in both English and French, decide which of the two you are more comfortable using; this will be considered your **first official language**. The other will be your **second official language**.

STEP 2. Determine your points according to your ability to read, write, listen to, and speak these languages using the criteria in the Canadian Language Benchmarks.

LANGUAGE ABILITY DOCUMENTATION

If you decide to apply to immigrate Canada as a skilled worker, you must provide **conclusive proof** of your language abilities. There are two ways to provide this proof. Choose **one** of the options below to establish your proficiency in English and/or French.

Option 1: take a language proficiency test

It is **strongly recommended** that you take a language test from an approved organization if you are claiming proficiency in a language that is **not** your native language. Language test results remain valid for one year.

Option 2: provide supporting documentation

If you believe that a language test is not necessary, you may establish your proficiency levels through a written explanation and supporting documentation. Your explanation and documents must **clearly** show that you meet the reading, writing, listening to and speaking criteria for the proficiency levels you are claiming in English and French, as they are listed in the Canadian Language Benchmarks.

Arranging a language test

If you choose Option 1, you must arrange a language test from any of the approved organizations. For contact information, refer to page: Language Proficiency Tests

Steps:

1 Make arrangements for testing and pay test costs.

2 Submit the assessment results with your immigration application.

Results:

• Test results will be used as conclusive evidence of your language proficiency.

• You will know **exactly** how many points you will receive for the language factor before you submit your application. To determine your points, see the test result equivalency charts that follow.

Steps:

1 Gather material that supports your claim. This should include:

   • A submission written by you that details your training in, and use of, English and/or French

   • Official documentation of education in English and/or French

   • Official documentation of work experience in English and/or French

2 Submit these documents with your immigration application. It is your responsibility to submit all documents; we will not contact you if information is missing.

Results:

• We will **not** interview you to assess your proficiency levels.

- If we are not satisfied of your claimed proficiency level, we may make our own assessment based on the information you submit. Your application may be refused if this results in a shortage of points.

- you will **not** know exactly how many points you will receive for the language factor until after we have assessed your application.

English language testing organizations:

The University of Cambridge Local Examination Syndicate, Education Australia, and the British Council administer the **International English Language Testing System (IELTS)**.

Note: IELTS has "General Training" and "Academic" options for the reading and writing tests. If you choose to take an IELTS test, you must take the "General Training" option.

The University of British Columbia's Applied Research and Evaluation Services (ARES) administer the **Canadian International Language Proficiency Index Program (CELPIP)**.

French language testing organizations:

The Paris Chamber of Commerce and Industry administers the **Test d'ÉÉvaluation de Français (TEF)**.

Note: For immigration purposes, you must submit results for the following tests:

- expression orale

- compréhension orale

- compréhension écrite

- expression écrite

FACTOR 3: WORK EXPERIENCE (MAXIMUM 21 POINTS)

Calculate your points by adding all of the years of full-time, paid work experience you have that:

- Occurred within the past 10 years

- Is **not** listed as a restricted occupation

- Occurred in occupations listed in Skill Type 0 or Skill Level A or B of the NOC

For points calculation, please see page: Point Grid

FACTOR 4: AGE (MAXIMUM 10 POINTS)

Points are given for your age at the time your application is received. See page: Point Grid for details.

FACTOR 5: ARRANGED EMPLOYMENT (MAXIMUM 10 POINTS)

If: You are currently working in Canada on a temporary work permit (including sectoral confirmations). And:

- Your work permit is valid for 12 or more months **after** the date you apply for a permanent resident visa;

- Your employer has made an offer to give you a permanent job if your application is successful. **10**

If: You are currently working in Canada in a job that is HRDC confirmation-exempt under an international agreement or a significant benefit category (e.g. intra-company transferee). And:

• Your work permit is valid for 12 or more months **after** the date you apply for a permanent resident visa;

• Your employer has made an offer to give you a permanent job if your application is successful. **10**

If: You do not currently have a work permit and you do not intend to work in Canada before you have been issued a permanent resident visa. And:

• You have a full-time job offer that has been confirmed by Human Resources Development Canada (HRDC);

• Your employer has made an offer to give you a permanent job if your application is successful.

• You meet all required Canadian licensing or regulatory standards associated with the job.

Note:

• You cannot arrange for an HRDC confirmation. Your employer must do this.

• HRDC will confirm job offers for occupations listed in Skill Type 0 or Skill Level A or B of the NOC. **10**

FACTOR 6: ADAPTABILITY (MAXIMUM 10 POINTS)

Points are awarded for certain adaptability elements based on the experience of the principal applicant and/or his or her spouse or common-law partner.

Instructions:

If you have a spouse or common-law partner, points for each element can be awarded only once, either for you **or** your spouse or common-law partner.

Adaptability criteria Points

A. Spouse or common-law partner's level of education

• Secondary school (high school) diploma or less: **0 points**

• A one-year diploma, trade certificate, apprenticeship, or university degree and at least 12 years of full-time or full-time equivalent studies: **3 points**

• A diploma, trade certificate, apprenticeship, or university degree of two years or more and at least 14 years of full-time or full-time equivalent studies: **4 points**

• A Master's or PhD and at least 17 years of full-time or full-time equivalent studies: **5 points**

B. Previous study in Canada:

• You or your accompanying spouse or common-law partner studied at a post-secondary institution in Canada for at least two years on a full-time basis. This must have been done after the age of 17 and with a valid study permit. **5 points**

C. Previous work in Canada:

• You or your accompanying spouse or common-law partner completed a minimum of one year of full-time work in Canada on a valid work permit. **5 points**

D. Arranged employment:

 • You earned points under Factor 5: Arranged Employment. **5 points**

E. Relatives in Canada:

 • You or your accompanying spouse or common-law partner has a relative (parent, grandparent, child, grandchild, child of a parent, sibling, child of a grandparent, aunt/uncle, or grandchild of a parent, niece or nephew) who lives in Canada and is a Canadian citizen or permanent resident. **5 points**

The pass mark:

The pass marks is 67 out of 100.

If: Your total score is equal to or greater than the pass mark...

Then:

 You may qualify for immigration to Canada as a skilled worker. Read the rest of this guide to decide if you wish to apply under the Federal Skilled Worker Class.

If: Your total score is less than the pass mark...

Then:

 • You are not likely to qualify for immigration to Canada as a skilled worker. We recommend that you do not apply at this time;

 • However, you may apply if you believe there are other factors that would help you to become economically established in Canada. Send a detailed letter with your application explaining these factors. Include any documents that support your claim.

Working in Canada:

Finding employment in Canada requires planning. You should obtain as much information as possible before you apply to immigrate. There is no guarantee that you will be able to work in your preferred occupation.

Although credential assessment and licensing are not requirements of the skilled worker application, you need to be aware of these issues when considering immigrating to Canada.

Regulated occupations

Twenty percent of people working in Canada work in occupations that are regulated to protect the health and safety of Canadians. Examples include nurses, engineers, electricians and teachers.

Provincial and territorial regulatory bodies are responsible for establishing entry requirements for individual occupations; for recognizing prior credentials, training and experience; and for issuing licences required to practice. The recognition process varies between provinces and territories and between occupations.

Recognition of qualifications and issuance of licenses can generally only be completed once in Canada. The process can take time. You may be asked to:

 • provide documentation of qualifications

 • undergo a language examination (which may differ from those required for immigration)

 • complete a technical exam (with accompanying fee)

 • do supervised work

Non-regulated occupations

For non-regulated occupations, there are no set requirements and there is no legal requirement to obtain a licence. The employer will set the standards and may very well request registration with a professional association.

Credential assessment

A credential assessment is advice on how qualifications from another country compare to Canadian qualifications. An assessment **does not** guarantee that:

• a regulatory body will issue you a licence to practice

• your credentials will be accepted by a Canadian employer

However, a credential assessment **will** help you understand the Canadian educational system and assist you with your job search.

You can have your credentials assessed by one of the provincial evaluation services.

Labour market information

Job opportunities and labour market conditions are different in each region of Canada. It is important to research conditions in the area in which you want to live. Follow the 'Working in Canada' link on our Web site for helpful sites on the Canadian labour market, job banks, and provincial and territorial labour market information.

MEDICAL REQUIREMENTS:

You and your family members, whether accompanying you or not, must undergo and pass a medical examination in order to come to Canada. To pass the medical examination you or your family members must not have a condition that:

• is a danger to public health or safety

• would cause excessive demand on health or social services in Canada. Examples of "excessive demand" include ongoing hospitalization or institutional care for a physical or mental illness.

Instructions

Instructions on how to undergo the medical examination will normally be sent to you after you submit your application to the visa office.

Exam validity

The medical examination results are valid for 12 months from the date of the first medical examination. If you are not admitted as a permanent resident during this time, you must undergo another complete medical examination.

Authorized doctors

Your own doctor cannot do the medical examination. You must see a physician on Canada's list of Panel Doctors. Note that the physician is only responsible for conducting a medical examination; he or she cannot give you any advice on the immigration process.

SECURITY REQUIREMENTS:

Police certificates and clearances

You and your family members must provide us with a police certificate issued by the authorities of each country in which you have lived for six (6) months or more since reaching the age of 18. Certificates must be originals and issued within the last three months.

If you have been convicted of a criminal offence in Canada, your application cannot be approved unless you receive a pardon. To avoid the unnecessary payment of processing fees for an immigration application that will be refused, you should first apply for a pardon to the:

Clemency and Pardons Division
National Parole Board
410 Laurier Avenue West
Ottawa, ON, Canada
K1A 0R1
Fax: 1-613-941-4981

Web site: www.npb-cnlc.gc.ca (application forms can be downloaded from the site)

Point Grid

Factor One: Education	Maximum 25
You have a Master's Degree or Ph.D. **and** at least 17 years of full-time or full-time equivalent study.	25
You have two or more university degrees at the bachelor's level **and** at least 15 years of full-time or full-time equivalent study.	22
You have a three-year diploma, trade certificate or apprenticeship **and** at least 15 years of full-time or full-time equivalent study.	22
You have a two-year university degree at the bachelor's level **and** at least 14 years of full-time or full-time equivalent study.	20
You have a two-year diploma, trade certificate or apprenticeship **and** at least 14 years of full-time or full-time equivalent study.	20
You have a one-year university degree at the bachelor's level **and** at least 13 years of full-time or full-time equivalent study.	15
You have a one-year diploma, trade certificate or apprenticeship **and** at least 13 years of full-time or full-time equivalent study.	15
You have a one-year diploma, trade certificate or apprenticeship **and** at least 12 years of full-time or full-time equivalent study.	12
You completed high school.	5

Factor Two: Official Languages	Maximum 24
1st Official Language	
High proficiency (per ability)	4
Moderate proficiency (per ability)	2
Basic proficiency (per ability)	1 to maximum of 2
No proficiency	0
Possible maximum (all 4 abilities)	16
2nd Official Language	
High proficiency (per ability)	2
Moderate proficiency (per ability)	2
Basic proficiency (per ability)	1 to maximum of 2

No proficiency	0
Possible maximum (all 4 abilities)	8
Factor Three: Experience	**Maximum 21**
1 year	15
2 years	17
3 years	19
4 years	21
Factor Four: Age	**Maximum 10**
21 to 49 years at time of application	10
Less 2 points for each year over 49 or under 21	
Factor Five: Arranged Employment In Canada	**Maximum 10**
You have a Human Resources Development Canada (HRDC) confirmed offer of permanent employment.	10
You are applying from within Canada and have a temporary work permit that is:	
HRDC confirmed, including sectoral confirmations; or	10
HRDC confirmation exempt under NAFTA, GATS, CCFTA, or significant economic benefit (i.e. intra-company transferee.)	10
Factor Six: Adaptability	**Maximum 10**
Spouse's or common-law partner's education	3 - 5
Minimum one year full-time authorized work in Canada	5
Minimum two years full-time authorized post-secondary study in Canada	5
Have received points under the Arranged Employment in Canada factor	5
Family relationship in Canada	5
Total	**Maximum 100**
Pass Mark	**67**

Funds Required

You must show that you have enough money to support yourself and your dependants after you arrive in Canada. You cannot borrow this money from another person. You must be able to use this money to support your family.

Number of Family Members	Funds Required (in Canadian dollars)
1	$10,168
2	$12,659
3	$15,563
4	$18,895
5	$21,431
6	$24,170
7 or more	$26,910

CITIZENSHIP AND IMMIGRATION CANADA
http://www.cic.gc.ca

Language Proficiency Tests

Approved Language Tests

You can arrange to take a language test from any of the following approved organizations:

English Tests

- International English Language Testing System (IELTS) General

- Canadian International Language Proficiency Index Program (CELPIP)

French Tests

- Test d'Evaluation de Francais (TEF)

Equivalency Charts

Once you have taken a language test from an approved organization, you can see how many points you will earn:

1. If you took an **International English Language Testing System (IELTS)** test;

2. If you took the **Canadian English Language Proficiency Index Program (CELPIP)**; or

3. If you took a **Test d'Evaluation de Francais**.

Test Score Equivalency Chart: International English Language Testing System

Level	Points (per ability)	Test Results for each Ability			
		Speaking	Listening	Reading	Writing
High (CLB/SLC 8-12)	First Official Language: **4**	7.0 - 9.0	7.0 - 9.0	7.0 - 9.0	7.0 - 9.0
	Second Official Language: **2**				
Moderate (CLB/SLC 6-7)	2	5.0 - 6.9	5.0 - 6.9	5.0 - 6.9	5.0 - 6.9
Basic (CLB/SLC 4-5)	1 (to a maximum of 2)	4.0 - 4.9	4.0 - 4.9	4.0 - 4.9	4.0 - 4.9
No (CLB/SLC 0-3)	0	Less than 4.0	Less than 4.0	Less than 4.0	Less than 4.0

Test Score Equivalency Chart: Canadian English Language Proficiency Index Program

Level	Points (per ability)	Test Results for each Ability			
		Speaking	Listening	Reading	Writing
High (CLB/SLC 8-12)	First Official Language: **4**	4H 5 6	4H 5 6	4H 5 6	4H 5 6
	Second Official Language: **2**				
Moderate (CLB/SLC 6-7)	**2**	3H 4L	3H 4L	3H 4L	3H 4L
Basic (CLB/SLC 4-5)	**1** (to a maximum of 2)	2H 3L	2H 3L	2H 3L	2H 3L
No (CLB/SLC 0-3)	**0**	0 1 2L	0 1 2L	0 1 2L	0 1 2L

Test Score Equivalency Chart: Test d'Evaluation de Francais

Level	Points (per ability)	Test Results for each Ability			
		Speaking	Listening	Reading	Writing
High (CLB/SLC 8-12)	First Official Language: **4**	Level 5 Level 6	Level 5 Level 6 (271-360 points)	Level 5 Level 6 (226-300 points)	Level 5 Level 6
	Second Official Language: **2**				
Moderate (CLB/SLC 6-7)	**2**	Level 4	Level 4 (199-270 points)	Level 4 (166-225 points)	Level 4
Basic (CLB/SLC 4-5)	**1** (to a maximum of 2)	Level 3	Level 3 (163-198 points)	Level 3 (136-165 points)	Level 3
No (CLB/SLC 0-3)	**0**	Level 0 Level 1 Level 2	Level 0 Level 1 Level 2 (0-162 points)	Level 0 Level 1 Level 2 (0-135 points)	Level 0 Level 1 Level 2

Skill Level A

<u>Major Group 11- Professional Occupations in Business and Finance</u>	**111 Auditors, Accountants and Investment Professionals** 1111 Financial Auditors and Accountants 1112 Financial and Investment Analysts http://www23.hrdc-drhc.gc.ca/2001/e/groups/1113.shtml 1113 Securities Agents, Investment Dealers and Brokers 1114 Other Financial Officers **112 Human Resources and Business Service Professionals** 1121 Specialists in Human Resources 1122 Professional Occupations in Business Services to Management
<u>Major Group 21 - Professional Occupations in Natural and Applied Sciences</u>	211 Physical Science Professionals 2111 Physicists and Astronomers 2112 Chemists 2113 Geologists, Geochemists and Geophysicists 2114 Meteorologists 2115 Other Professional Occupations in Physical Sciences **212 Life Science Professionals** 2121 Biologists and Related Scientists 2122 Forestry Professionals 2123 Agricultural Representatives, Consultants and Specialists **213 Civil, Mechanical, Electrical and Chemical Engineers** 2131 Civil Engineers 2132 Mechanical Engineers 2133 Electrical and Electronics Engineers 2134 Chemical Engineers **214 Other Engineers** 2141 Industrial and Manufacturing Engineers 2142 Metallurgical and Materials Engineers 2143 Mining Engineers 2144 Geological Engineers 2145 Petroleum Engineers 2146 Aerospace Engineers 2147 Computer Engineers (Except Software Engineers) 2148 Other Professional Engineers, n.e.c. **215 Architects, Urban Planners and Land Surveyors** 2151 Architects 2152 Landscape Architects 2153 Urban and Land Use Planners 2154 Land Surveyors **216 Mathematicians, Statisticians and Actuaries** 2161 Mathematicians, Statisticians and Actuaries **217 Computer and Information Systems Professionals** 2171 Information Systems Analysts and Consultants 2172 Database Analysts and Data Administrators

	2173 Software Engineers 2174 Computer Programmers and Interactive Media Developers 2175 Web Designers and Developers
Major Group 31 - Professional Occupations in Health	311 Physicians, Dentists and Veterinarians 3112 General Practitioners and Family Physicians 3113 Dentists 3114 Veterinarians **312 Optometrists, Chiropractors and Other Health Diagnosing and Treating Professionals** 3121 Optometrists 3122 Chiropractors 3123 Other Professional Occupations in Health Diagnosing and Treating **313 Pharmacists, Dietitians and Nutritionists** 3131 Pharmacists 3132 Dietitians and Nutritionists **314 Therapy and Assessment Professionals** 3141 Audiologists and Speech-Language Pathologists 3142 Physiotherapists 3143 Occupational Therapists 3144 Other Professional Occupations in Therapy and Assessment **315 Nurse Supervisors and Registered Nurses** 3151 Head Nurses and Supervisors 3152 Registered Nurses
Major Group 41 - Professional Occupations in Social Science, Education, Government Services and Religion	411 Judges, Lawyers and Quebec Notaries 4111 Judges 4112 Lawyers and Quebec Notaries **412 University Professors and Assistants** 4121 University Professors 4122 Post-Secondary Teaching and Research Assistants **413 College and Other Vocational Instructors** 4131 College and Other Vocational Instructors **414 Secondary and Elementary School Teachers and Educational Counsellors** 4141 Secondary School Teachers 4142 Elementary School and Kindergarten Teachers 4143 Educational Counsellors **415 Psychologists, Social Workers, Counsellors, Clergy and Probation Officers** 4151 Psychologists 4152 Social Workers 4153 Family, Marriage and Other Related Counsellors 4154 Ministers of Religion 4155 Probation and Parole Officers and Related Occupations

	416 Policy and Program Officers, Researchers and Consultants
	<u>4161</u> Natural and Applied Science Policy Researchers, Consultants and Program Officers
	<u>4162</u> Economists and Economic Policy Researchers and Analysts
	<u>4163</u> Business Development Officers and Marketing Researchers and Consultants
	<u>4164</u> Social Policy Researchers, Consultants and Program Officers
	<u>4165</u> Health Policy Researchers, Consultants and Program Officers
	<u>4166</u> Education Policy Researchers, Consultants and Program Officers
	<u>4167</u> Recreation, Sports and Fitness Program Supervisors Consultants
	<u>4168</u> Program Officers Unique to Government
	<u>4169</u> Other Professional Occupations in Social Science, n.e.c.
<u>Major Group 51 - Professional Occupations in Art and Culture</u>	511 Librarians, Archivists, Conservators and Curators
	<u>5111</u> Librarians
	<u>5112</u> Conservators and Curators
	<u>5113</u> Archivists
	512 Writing, Translating and Public Relations Professionals
	<u>5121</u> Authors and Writers
	<u>5122</u> Editors
	<u>5123</u> Journalists
	<u>5124</u> Professional Occupations in Public Relations and Communications
	<u>5125</u> Translators, Terminologists and Interpreters
	513 Creative and Performing Artists
	<u>5131</u> Producers, Directors, Choreographers and Related Occupations
	<u>5132</u> Conductors, Composers and Arrangers
	<u>5133</u> Musicians and Singers
	<u>5134</u> Dancers
	<u>5135</u> Actors and Comedians
	<u>5136</u> Painters, Sculptors and Other Visual Artists

Skill Level B

<u>**Major Group 12 -**</u> <u>**Skilled Administrative**</u> <u>**and Business**</u> <u>**Occupations**</u>	121 Clerical Supervisors 1211 Supervisors, General Office and Administrative Support Clerks 1212 Supervisors, Finance and Insurance Clerks 1213 Supervisors, Library, Correspondence and Related Information Clerks 1214 Supervisors, Mail and Message Distribution Occupations 1215 Supervisors, Recording, Distributing and Scheduling Occupations 122 Administrative and Regulatory Occupations 1221 Administrative Officers 1222 Executive Assistants 1223 Personnel and Recruitment Officers 1224 Property Administrators 1225 Purchasing Agents and Officers 1226 Conference and Event Planners 1227 Court Officers and Justices of the Peace 1228 Immigration, Employment Insurance and Revenue Officers 123 Finance and Insurance Administrative Occupations 1231 Bookkeepers 1232 Loan Officers 1233 Insurance Adjusters and Claims Examiners 1234 Insurance Underwriters 1235 Assessors, Valuators and Appraisers 1236 Customs, Ship and Other Brokers 124 Secretaries, Recorders and Transcriptionists 1241 Secretaries (Except Legal and Medical) 1242 Legal Secretaries 1243 Medical Secretaries 1244 Court Recorders and Medical Transcriptionists
<u>**Major Group 22 -**</u> <u>**Technical Occupations**</u> <u>**Related to Natural and**</u> <u>**Applied Sciences**</u>	221 Technical Occupations in Physical Sciences **2211** Chemical Technologists and Technicians **2212** Geological and Mineral Technologists and Technicians **2213** Meteorological Technicians 222 Technical Occupations in Life Sciences **2221** Biological Technologists and Technicians **2222** Agricultural and Fish Products Inspectors **2223** Forestry Technologists and Technicians **2224** Conservation and Fishery Officers **2225** Landscape and Horticultural Technicians and Specialists 223 Technical Occupations in Civil, Mechanical and Industrial Engineering **2231** Civil Engineering Technologists and Technicians **2232** Mechanical Engineering Technologists and Technicians **2233** Industrial Engineering and Manufacturing Technologists and Technicians **2234** Construction Estimators 224 Technical Occupations in Electronics and Electrical Engineering **2241** Electrical and Electronics Engineering Technologists and Technicians **2242** Electronic Service Technicians (Household and Business **2243** Industrial Instrument Technicians and Mechanics **2244** Aircraft Instrument, Electrical and Avionics Mechanics, Technicians and Inspectors 225 Technical Occupations in Architecture, Drafting, Surveying and Mapping

	2251 Architectural Technologists and Technicians 2252 Industrial Designers 2253 Drafting Technologists and Technicians 2254 Land Survey Technologists and Technicians 2255 Mapping and Related Technologists and Technicians 226 Other Technical Inspectors and Regulatory Officers 2261 Nondestructive Testers and Inspectors 2262 Engineering Inspectors and Regulatory Officers 2263 Inspectors in Public and Environmental Health and Occupational Health and Safety 2264 Construction Inspectors 227 Transportation Officers and Controllers 2271 Air Pilots, Flight Engineers and Flying Instructors 2272 Air Traffic Control and Related Occupations 2273 Deck Officers, Water Transport 2274 Engineer Officers, Water Transport 2275 Railway Traffic Controllers and Marine Traffic Regulators 228 Technical Occupations in Computer and Information Systems 2281 Computer and Network Operators and Web Technicians 2282 User Support Technicians 2283 Systems Testing Technicians
Major Group 32 - Technical and Skilled Occupations in Health	321 Medical Technologists and Technicians (Except Dental Health) 3211 Medical Laboratory Technologists and Pathologists' Assistants 3212 Medical Laboratory Technicians 3213 Veterinary and Animal Health Technologists and 3214 Respiratory Therapists, Clinical Perfusionists and Cardio-Pulmonary Technologists 3215 Medical Radiation Technologists 3216 Medical Sonographers 3217 Cardiology Technologists 3218 Electroencephalographic and Other Diagnostic Technologists, n.e.c. 3219 Other Medical Technologists and Technicians (Except Dental Health) 322 Technical Occupations in Dental Health Care 3221 Denturists 3222 Dental Hygienists and Dental Therapists 3223 Dental Technologists, Technicians and Laboratory 323 Other Technical Occupations in Health Care (Except Dental) 3231 Opticians 3232 Midwives and Practitioners of Natural Healing 3233 Licensed Practical Nurses 3234 Ambulance Attendants and Other Paramedical Occupations 3235 Other Technical Occupations in Therapy and Assessment
Major Group 42 - Paraprofessional Occupations in Law, Social Services, Education and Religion	421 Paralegals, Social Services Workers and Occupations in Education and Religion, n.e.c. 4211 Paralegal and Related Occupations 4212 Community and Social Service Workers 4213 Employment Counsellors 4214 Early Childhood Educators and Assistants 4215 Instructors and Teachers of Persons with Disabilities 4216 Other Instructors 4217 Other Religious Occupations
Major Group 52 - Technical and Skilled Occupations in Art, Culture, Recreation and	521 Technical Occupations in Libraries, Archives, Museums and Art Galleries 5211 Library and Archive Technicians and Assistants 5212 Technical Occupations Related to Museums and Art Galleries

Sport	522 Photographers, Graphic Arts Technicians and Technical and Co-ordinating Occupations in Motion Pictures, Broadcasting and the Performing Arts **5221** Photographers **5222** Film and Video Camera Operators **5223** Graphic Arts Technicians **5224** Broadcast Technicians **5225** Audio and Video Recording Technicians **5226** Other Technical and Co-ordinating Occupations in Motion Pictures, Broadcasting **5227** Support Occupations in Motion Pictures, Broadcasting and the Performing Arts 523 Announcers and Other Performers **5231** Announcers and Other Broadcasters **5232** Other Performers 524 Creative Designers and Craftspersons **5241** Graphic Designers and Illustrators **5242** Interior Designers **5243** Theatre, Fashion, Exhibit and Other Creative Designers **5244** Artisans and Craftpersons **5245** Patternmakers - Textile, Leather and Fur Products 525 Athletes, Coaches, Referees and Related Occupations **5251** Athletes **5252** Coaches **5253** Sports Officials and Referees **5254** Program Leaders and Instructors in Recreation and Sport
<u>Major Group 62 - Skilled Sales and Service Occupations</u>	621 Sales and Service Supervisors **6211** Retail Trade Supervisors **6212** Food Service Supervisors **6213** Executive Housekeepers **6214** Dry Cleaning and Laundry Supervisors **6215** Cleaning Supervisors **6216** Other Service Supervisors 622 Technical Sales Specialists, Wholesale Trade **6221** Technical Sales Specialists - Wholesale Trade 623 Insurance and Real Estate Sales Occupations and Buyers **6231** Insurance Agents and Brokers **6232** Real Estate Agents and Salespersons **6233** Retail and Wholesale Buyers **6234** Grain Elevator Operators 624 Chefs and Cooks **6241** Chefs **6242** Cooks 625 Butchers and Bakers **6251** Butchers and Meat Cutters - Retail and Wholesale **6252** Bakers 626 Police Officers and Firefighters **6261** Police Officers (Except Commissioned) **6262** Firefighters 627 Technical Occupations in Personal Service **6271** Hairstylists and Barbers **6272** Funeral Directors and Embalmers

Major Group 72-73 - Trades and Skilled Transport and Equipment Operators	721 Contractors and Supervisors, Trades and Related Workers

721 Contractors and Supervisors, Trades and Related Workers

7211 Supervisors, Machinists and Related Occupations
7212 Contractors and Supervisors, Electrical Trades and Telecommunications
7213 Contractors and Supervisors, Pipefitting Trades
7214 Contractors and Supervisors, Metal Forming, Shaping and Erecting Trades
7215 Contractors and Supervisors, Carpentry Trades
7216 Contractors and Supervisors, Mechanic Trades
7217 Contractors and Supervisors, Heavy Construction Equipment Crews
7218 Supervisors, Printing and Related Occupations
7219 Contractors and Supervisors, Other Construction Trades, Installers, Repairers

722 Supervisors, Railway and Motor Transportation Occupations

7221 Supervisors, Railway Transport Operations
7222 Supervisors, Motor Transport and Other Ground Transit Operators

723 Machinists and Related Occupations

7231 Machinists and Machining and Tooling Inspectors
7232 Tool and Die Makers

724 Electrical Trades and Telecommunication Occupations

7241 Electricians (Except Industrial and Power System)
7242 Industrial Electricians
7243 Power System Electricians
7244 Electrical Power Line and Cable Workers
7245 Telecommunications Line and Cable Workers
7246 Telecommunications Installation and Repair Workers
7247 Cable Television Service and Maintenance Technicians

725 Plumbers, Pipefitters and Gas Fitters

7251 Plumbers
7252 Steamfitters, Pipefitters and Sprinkler System Installers
7253 Gas Fitters

726 Metal Forming, Shaping and Erecting Trades

7261 Sheet Metal Workers
7262 Boilermakers
7263 Structural Metal and Platework Fabricators and Fitters
7264 Ironworkers
7265 Welders and Related Machine Operators
7266 Blacksmiths and Die Setters

727 Carpenters and Cabinetmakers

7271 Carpenters
7272 Cabinetmakers

728 Masonry and Plastering Trades

7281 Bricklayers
7283 Tilesetters
7284 Plasterers, Drywall Installers and Finishers and Lathers

729 Other Construction Trades

7291 Roofers and Shinglers
7292 Glaziers
7293 Insulators
7294 Painters and Decorators
7295 Floor Covering Installers

731 Machinery and Transportation Equipment Mechanics (Except Motor Vehicle)

7311 Construction Millwrights and Industrial Mechanics (Except Textile)
7312 Heavy-Duty Equipment Mechanics
7313 Refrigeration and Air Conditioning Mechanics
7314 Railway Carmen/women
7315 Aircraft Mechanics and Aircraft Inspectors

7316 Machine Fitters
7317 Textile Machinery Mechanics and Repairers
7318 Elevator Constructors and Mechanics

732 Automotive Service Technicians

7321 Automotive Service Technicians, Truck Mechanics and Mechanical Repairers
7322 Motor Vehicle Body Repairers

733 Other Mechanics

7331 Oil and Solid Fuel Heating Mechanics
7332 Electric Appliance Servicers and Repairers
7333 Electrical Mechanics
7334 Motorcycle and Other Related Mechanics
7335 Other Small Engine and Equipment Mechanics

734 Upholsterers, Tailors, Shoe Repairers, Jewellers and Related Occupations

7341 Upholsterers
7342 Tailors, Dressmakers, Furriers and Milliners
7343 Shoe Repairers and Shoemakers
7344 Jewellers, Watch Repairers and Related Occupations

735 Stationary Engineers and Power Station and System Operators

7351 Stationary Engineers and Auxiliary Equipment Operators
7352 Power Systems and Power Station Operators

736 Train Crew Operating Occupations

7361 Railway and Yard Locomotive Engineers
7362 Railway Conductors and Brakemen/women

737 Crane Operators, Drillers and Blasters

7371 Crane Operators
7372 Drillers and Blasters Ð Surface Mining, Quarrying and Construction
7373 Water Well Drillers

738 Printing Press Operators, Commercial Divers and Other Trades and Related Occupations, n.e.c.

7381 Printing Press Operators
7382 Commercial Divers
7383 Other Trades and Related Occupations

<u>Major Group 82 - Skilled Occupations in Primary Industry</u>	821 Supervisors, Logging and Forestry **8211** Supervisors, Logging and Forestry 822 Supervisors, Mining, Oil and Gas **8221** Supervisors, Mining and Quarrying **8222** Supervisors, Oil and Gas Drilling and Service 823 Underground Miners, Oil and Gas Drillers and Related Workers **8231** Underground Production and Development Miners **8232** Oil and Gas Well Drillers, Servicers, Testers and Related Workers 824 Logging Machinery Operators **8241** Logging Machinery Operators 825 Contractors, Operators and Supervisors in Agriculture, Horticulture and Aquaculture **8251** Farmers and Farm Managers **8252** Agricultural and Related Service Contractors and Managers **8253** Farm Supervisors and Specialized Livestock Workers **8254** Nursery and Greenhouse Operators and Managers **8255** Landscaping and Grounds Maintenance Contractors and Managers

	8256 Supervisors, Landscape and Horticulture **8257** Aquaculture Operators and Managers 826 Fishing Vessel Masters and Skippers and Fishermen/women **8261** Fishing Masters and Officers **8262** Fishing Vessel Skippers and Fishermen/women
<u>Major Group 92 - Processing, Manufacturing and Utilities Supervisors and Skilled Operators</u>	921 Supervisors, Processing Occupations **9211** Supervisors, Mineral and Metal Processing **9212** Supervisors, Petroleum, Gas and Chemical Processing and Utilities **9213** Supervisors, Food, Beverage and Tobacco Processing **9214** Supervisors, Plastic and Rubber Products Manufacturing **9215** Supervisors, Forest Products Processing **9216** Supervisors, Textile Processing 922 Supervisors, Assembly and Fabrication **9221** Supervisors, Motor Vehicle Assembling **9222** Supervisors, Electronics Manufacturing **9223** Supervisors, Electrical Products Manufacturing **9224** Supervisors, Furniture and Fixtures Manufacturing **9225** Supervisors, Fabric, Fur and Leather Products Manufacturing **9226** Supervisors, Other Mechanical and Metal Products Manufacturing **9227** Supervisors, Other Products Manufacturing and Assembly 923 Central Control and Process Operators in Manufacturing and Processing **9231** Central Control and Process Operators, Mineral and Metal Processing **9232** Petroleum, Gas and Chemical Process Operators **9233** Pulping Control Operators **9234** Papermaking and Coating Control Operators

Skill Level 0

<u>Major Group 00 - Senior Management Occupations</u>	**001 Legislators and Senior Management** <u>0011</u> Legislators <u>0012</u> Senior Government Managers and Officials <u>0013</u> Senior Managers - Financial, Communications and Other Business <u>0014</u> Senior Managers - Health, Education, Social and Community <u>0015</u> Senior Managers - Trade, Broadcasting and Other Services, n.e.c. <u>0016</u> Senior Managers - Goods Production, Utilities, Transportation and Construction
<u>Major Group 01-09 - Middle and Other Management Occupations</u>	**011 Administrative Services Managers** <u>0111</u> Financial Managers <u>0112</u> Human Resources Managers <u>0113</u> Purchasing Managers <u>0114</u> Other Administrative Services Managers **012 Managers in Financial and Business Services** <u>0121</u> Insurance, Real Estate and Financial Brokerage Managers <u>0122</u> Banking, Credit and Other Investment Managers <u>0123</u> Other Business Services Managers **013 Managers in Communication (Except Broadcasting)** <u>0131</u> Telecommunication Carriers Managers <u>0132</u> Postal and Courier Services Managers **021 Managers in Engineering, Architecture, Science and Information Systems** <u>0211</u> Engineering Managers <u>0212</u> Architecture and Science Managers <u>0213</u> Computer and Information Systems Managers **031 Managers in Health, Education, Social and Community Services** <u>0311</u> Managers in Health Care <u>0312</u> Administrators - Post-Secondary Education and Vocational <u>0313</u> School Principals and Administrators of Elementary and Secondary <u>0314</u> Managers in Social, Community and Correctional Services **041 Managers in Public Administration** <u>0411</u> Government Managers - Health and Social Policy Development and Program Administration <u>0412</u> Government Managers - Economic Analysis, Policy Development <u>0413</u> Government Managers - Education Policy Development and Program Administration <u>0414</u> Other Managers in Public Administration **051 Managers in Art, Culture, Recreation and Sport** <u>0511</u> Library, Archive, Museum and Art Gallery Managers <u>0512</u> Managers - Publishing, Motion Pictures, Broadcasting and Performing Arts <u>0513</u> Recreation and Sports Program and Service Directors **061 Sales, Marketing and Advertising Managers** <u>0611</u> Sales, Marketing and Advertising Managers

062 Managers in Retail Trade

0621 Retail Trade Managers

063 Managers in Food Service and Accommodation

0631 Restaurant and Food Service Managers
0632 Accommodation Service Managers

064 Managers in Protective Service

0641 Commissioned Police Officers
0642 Fire Chiefs and Senior Firefighting Officers
0643 Commissioned Officers, Armed Forces

065 Managers in Other Services

0651 Other Services Managers

071 Managers in Construction and Transportation

0711 Construction Managers
0712 Residential Home Builders and Renovators
0713 Transportation Managers

072 Facility Operation and Maintenance Managers

0721 Facility Operation and Maintenance Managers

081 Managers in Primary Production (Except Agriculture)

0811 Primary Production Managers (Except Agriculture)

091 Managers in Manufacturing and Utilities

0911 Manufacturing Managers
0912 Utilities Managers

Occupational List

Code	A
0632	Accommodation Service Managers
5135	Actors and Comedians
1221	Administrative Officers
0114	Administrative Services Managers (other)
0312	Administrators - Post-Secondary Education and Vocational
2146	Aerospace Engineers
2222	Agricultural and Fish Products Inspectors
8252	Agricultural and Related Service Contractors and Managers
2123	Agricultural Representatives, Consultants and Specialists
2271	Air Pilots, Flight Engineers and Flying Instructors
2272	Air Traffic Control and Related Occupations
2244	Aircraft Instrument, Electrical and Avionics Mechanics, Technicians and Inspectors
7315	Aircraft Mechanics and Aircraft Inspectors
3234	Ambulance Attendants and Other Paramedical Occupations
5231	Announcers and Other Broadcasters
8257	Aquaculture Operators and Managers
2151	Architects
2251	Architectural Technologists and Technicians
0212	Architecture and Science Managers
5113	Archivists
5244	Artisans and Craftpersons
1235	Assessors, Valuators and Appraisers
5251	Athletes
5225	Audio and Video Recording Technicians
3141	Audiologists and Speech-Language Pathologists
5121	Authors and Writers
7321	Automotive Service Technicians, Truck Mechanics and Mechanical Repairers
Code	**B**
6252	Bakers
0122	Banking, Credit and Other Investment Managers
2221	Biological Technologists and Technicians
2121	Biologists and Related Scientists
7266	Blacksmiths and Die Setters
7262	Boilermakers
1231	Bookkeepers
7281	Bricklayers
5224	Broadcast Technicians
4163	Business Development Officers and Marketing Researchers and Consultants
0123	Business Services Managers (other)
6251	Butchers and Meat Cutters - Retail and Wholesale
Code	**C**

7272	Cabinetmakers
7247	Cable Television Service and Maintenance Technicians
3217	Cardiology Technologists
7271	Carpenters
9231	Central Control and Process Operators, Mineral and Metal Processing
6241	Chefs
2134	Chemical Engineers
2211	Chemical Technologists and Technicians
2112	Chemists
3122	Chiropractors
2231	Civil Engineering Technologists and Technicians
2131	Civil Engineers
6215	Cleaning Supervisors
5252	Coaches
4131	College and Other Vocational Instructors
7382	Commercial Divers
0643	Commissioned Officers, Armed Forces
0641	Commissioned Police Officers
4212	Community and Social Service Workers
0213	Computer and Information Systems Managers
2281	Computer and Network Operators and Web Technicians
2147	Computer Engineers (Except Software Engineers)
2174	Computer Programmers and Interactive Media Developers
7282	Concrete Finishers
5132	Conductors, Composers and Arrangers
1226	Conference and Event Planners
2224	Conservation and Fishery Officers
5112	Conservators and Curators
2234	Construction Estimators
2264	Construction Inspectors
0711	Construction Managers
7311	Construction Millwrights and Industrial Mechanics (Except Textile)
7215	Contractors and Supervisors, Carpentry Trades
7212	Contractors and Supervisors, Electrical Trades and Telecommunications
7217	Contractors and Supervisors, Heavy Construction Equipment Crews
7216	Contractors and Supervisors, Mechanic Trades
7214	Contractors and Supervisors, Metal Forming, Shaping and Erecting Trades
7219	Contractors and Supervisors, Other Construction Trades, Installers, Repairers
7213	Contractors and Supervisors, Pipefitting Trades
6242	Cooks
1227	Court Officers and Justices of the Peace
1244	Court Recorders and Medical Transcriptionists
7371	Crane Operators
1236	Customs, Ship and Other Brokers
Code	**D**
5134	Dancers
2172	Database Analysts and Data Administrators

2273	Deck Officers, Water Transport
3222	Dental Hygienists and Dental Therapists
3223	Dental Technologists, Technicians and Laboratory
3113	Dentists
3221	Denturists
3132	Dietitians and Nutritionists
2253	Drafting Technologists and Technicians
7372	Drillers and Blasters D Surface Mining, Quarrying and Construction
6214	Dry Cleaning and Laundry Supervisors
Code	**E**
4214	Early Childhood Educators and Assistants
4162	Economists and Economic Policy Researchers and Analysts
5122	Editors
4166	Education Policy Researchers, Consultants and Program Officers
4143	Educational Counsellors
7332	Electric Appliance Servicers and Repairers
2241	Electrical and Electronics Engineering Technologists and Technicians
2133	Electrical and Electronics Engineers
7333	Electrical Mechanics
7244	Electrical Power Line and Cable Workers
7241	Electricians (Except Industrial and Power System)
3218	Electroencephalographic and Other Diagnostic Technologists, n.e.c.
2242	Electronic Service Technicians (Household and Business
7318	Elevator Constructors and Mechanics
4213	Employment Counsellors
2274	Engineer Officers, Water Transport
2262	Engineering Inspectors and Regulatory Officers
0211	Engineering Managers
1222	Executive Assistants
6213	Executive Housekeepers
Code	**F**
0721	Facility Operation and Maintenance Managers
4153	Family, Marriage and Other Related Counsellors
8253	Farm Supervisors and Specialized Livestock Workers
8251	Farmers and Farm Managers
5222	Film and Video Camera Operators
1112	Financial and Investment Analysts
1111	Financial Auditors and Accountants
0111	Financial Managers
1114	Financial Officers (other)
0642	Fire Chiefs and Senior Firefighting Officers
6262	Firefighters
8261	Fishing Masters and Officers
8262	Fishing Vessel Skippers and Fishermen/women
7295	Floor Covering Installers
6212	Food Service Supervisors
2122	Forestry Professionals
2223	Forestry Technologists and Technicians

6272	Funeral Directors and Embalmers
Code	**G**
7253	Gas Fitters
2212	Geological and Mineral Technologists and Technicians
2144	Geological Engineers
2113	Geologists, Geochemists and Geophysicists
7292	Glaziers
0412	Government Managers - Economic Analysis, Policy Development
0413	Government Managers - Education Policy Development and Program Administration
0411	Government Managers - Health and Social Policy Development and Program Administration
6234	Grain Elevator Operators
5223	Graphic Arts Technicians
5241	Graphic Designers and Illustrators
Code	**H**
6271	Hairstylists and Barbers
3151	Head Nurses and Supervisors
3123	Health Diagnosing and Treating (Other Professional Occupations)
4165	Health Policy Researchers, Consultants and Program Officers
7312	Heavy-Duty Equipment Mechanics
0112	Human Resources Managers
Code	**I**
1228	Immigration, Employment Insurance and Revenue Officers
2141	Industrial and Manufacturing Engineers
2252	Industrial Designers
7242	Industrial Electricians
2233	Industrial Engineering and Manufacturing Technologists and Technicians
2243	Industrial Instrument Technicians and Mechanics
2171	Information Systems Analysts and Consultants
2263	Inspectors in Public and Environmental Health and Occupational Health and Safety
4216	Instructors (other)
4215	Instructors and Teachers of Persons with Disabilities
7293	Insulators
1233	Insurance Adjusters and Claims Examiners
6231	Insurance Agents and Brokers
1234	Insurance Underwriters
0121	Insurance, Real Estate and Financial Brokerage Managers
5242	Interior Designers
7264	Ironworkers
Code	**J**
7344	Jewellers, Watch Repairers and Related Occupations
5123	Journalists
4111	Judges
1227	Justices of the Peace
Code	**L**
2254	Land Survey Technologists and Technicians

2154	Land Surveyors
2225	Landscape and Horticultural Technicians and Specialists
2152	Landscape Architects
8255	Landscaping and Grounds Maintenance Contractors and Managers
4112	Lawyers and Quebec Notaries
1242	Legal Secretaries
0011	Legislators
5111	Librarians
5211	Library and Archive Technicians and Assistants
0511	Library, Archive, Museum and Art Gallery Managers
3233	Licensed Practical Nurses
1232	Loan Officers
8241	Logging Machinery Operators
Code	**M**
7316	Machine Fitters
7231	Machinists and Machining and Tooling Inspectors
0512	Managers - Publishing, Motion Pictures, Broadcasting and Performing Arts
0311	Managers in Health Care
0414	Managers in Public Administration (other)
0314	Managers in Social, Community and Correctional Services
0911	Manufacturing Managers
2255	Mapping and Related Technologists and Technicians
2161	Mathematicians, Statisticians and Actuaries
2232	Mechanical Engineering Technologists and Technicians
2132	Mechanical Engineers
3212	Medical Laboratory Technicians
3211	Medical Laboratory Technologists and Pathologists' Assistants
3215	Medical Radiation Technologists
1243	Medical Secretaries
3216	Medical Sonographers
3219	Medical Technologists and Technicians (other - except Dental Health)
2142	Metallurgical and Materials Engineers
2213	Meteorological Technicians
2114	Meteorologists
3232	Midwives and Practitioners of Natural Healing
2143	Mining Engineers
4154	Ministers of Religion
5226	Motion Pictures, Broadcasting (other Technical and Co-ordinating Occupations)
7322	Motor Vehicle Body Repairers
7334	Motorcycle and Other Related Mechanics
5212	Museums and Art Galleries (related Technical Occupations)
5133	Musicians and Singers
Code	**N**
4161	Natural and Applied Science Policy Researchers, Consultants and Program Officers
2261	Nondestructive Testers and Inspectors
8254	Nursery and Greenhouse Operators and Managers

Code	O
3143	Occupational Therapists
8232	Oil and Gas Well Drillers, Servicers, Testers and Related Workers
7331	Oil and Solid Fuel Heating Mechanics
3231	Opticians
3121	Optometrists
Code	P
7294	Painters and Decorators
5136	Painters, Sculptors and Other Visual Artists
9234	Papermaking and Coating Control Operators
4211	Paralegal and Related Occupations
5245	Patternmakers - Textile, Leather and Fur Products
5232	Performers (other)
1223	Personnel and Recruitment Officers
2145	Petroleum Engineers
9232	Petroleum, Gas and Chemical Process Operators
3131	Pharmacists
5221	Photographers
2115	Physical Sciences (Other Professional Occupations)
3112	Physicians - General Practitioners and Family Physicians
3111	Physicians - Specialist
2111	Physicists and Astronomers
3142	Physiotherapists
7252	Pipefitters
7284	Plasterers, Drywall Installers and Finishers and Lathers
7251	Plumbers
6261	Police Officers (Except Commissioned)
0132	Postal and Courier Services Managers
4122	Post-Secondary Teaching and Research Assistants
7243	Power System Electricians
7352	Power Systems and Power Station Operators
0811	Primary Production Managers (Except Agriculture)
7381	Printing Press Operators
4155	Probation and Parole Officers and Related Occupations
5131	Producers, Directors, Choreographers and Related Occupations
2148	Professional Engineers, n.e.c. (other)
1122	Professional Occupations in Business Services to Management
5124	Professional Occupations in Public Relations and Communications
4121	Professors - University
5254	Program Leaders and Instructors in Recreation and Sport
4168	Program Officers Unique to Government
1224	Property Administrators
4151	Psychologists
9233	Pulping Control Operators
1225	Purchasing Agents and Officers
0113	Purchasing Managers
Code	R
7361	Railway and Yard Locomotive Engineers

7314	Railway Carmen/women
7362	Railway Conductors and Brakemen/women
2275	Railway Traffic Controllers and Marine Traffic Regulators
6232	Real Estate Agents and Salespersons
0513	Recreation and Sports Program and Service Directors
4167	Recreation, Sports and Fitness Program Supervisors Consultants
7313	Refrigeration and Air Conditioning Mechanics
3152	Registered Nurses
4217	Religious Occupations (other)
0712	Residential Home Builders and Renovators
3214	Respiratory Therapists, Clinical Perfusionists and Cardio-Pulmonary Technologists
0631	Restaurant and Food Service Managers
6233	Retail and Wholesale Buyers
0621	Retail Trade Managers
6211	Retail Trade Supervisors
7291	Roofers and Shinglers
Code	**S**
0611	Sales, Marketing and Advertising Managers
0313	School Principals and Administrators of Elementary and Secondary
1241	Secretaries (Except Legal and Medical)
1113	Securities Agents, Investment Dealers and Brokers
0012	Senior Government Managers and Officials
0013	Senior Managers - Financial, Communications and Other Business
0016	Senior Managers - Goods Production, Utilities, Transportation and Construction
0014	Senior Managers - Health, Education, Social and Community
0015	Senior Managers - Trade, Broadcasting and Other Services, n.e.c.
6216	Service Supervisors (other)
0651	Services Managers (other)
7261	Sheet Metal Workers
7343	Shoe Repairers and Shoemakers
7335	Small Engine and Equipment Mechanics (other)
4164	Social Policy Researchers, Consultants and Program Officers
4169	Social Science, n.e.c. (Other Professional Occupations)
4152	Social Workers
2173	Software Engineers
1121	Specialists in Human Resources
5253	Sports Officials and Referees
7252	Sprinkler System Installers
7351	Stationary Engineers and Auxiliary Equipment Operators
7252	Steamfitters, Pipefitters and Sprinkler System Installers
7263	Structural Metal and Platework Fabricators and Fitters
9223	Supervisors, Electrical Products Manufacturing
9222	Supervisors, Electronics Manufacturing
9225	Supervisors, Fabric, Fur and Leather Products Manufacturing
1212	Supervisors, Finance and Insurance Clerks
9213	Supervisors, Food, Beverage and Tobacco Processing
9215	Supervisors, Forest Products Processing

9224	Supervisors, Furniture and Fixtures Manufacturing
1211	Supervisors, General Office and Administrative Support Clerks
8256	Supervisors, Landscape and Horticulture
1213	Supervisors, Library, Correspondence and Related Information Clerks
8211	Supervisors, Logging and Forestry
7211	Supervisors, Machinists and Related Occupations
1214	Supervisors, Mail and Message Distribution Occupations
9211	Supervisors, Mineral and Metal Processing
8221	Supervisors, Mining and Quarrying
7222	Supervisors, Motor Transport and Other Ground Transit Operators
9221	Supervisors, Motor Vehicle Assembling
8222	Supervisors, Oil and Gas Drilling and Service
9226	Supervisors, Other Mechanical and Metal Products Manufacturing
9227	Supervisors, Other Products Manufacturing and Assembly
9212	Supervisors, Petroleum, Gas and Chemical Processing and Utilities
9214	Supervisors, Plastic and Rubber Products Manufacturing
7218	Supervisors, Printing and Related Occupations
7221	Supervisors, Railway Transport Operations
1215	Supervisors, Recording, Distributing and Scheduling Occupations
9216	Supervisors, Textile Processing
5227	Support Occupations in Motion Pictures, Broadcasting and the Performing Arts
2283	Systems Testing Technicians
Code	**T**
7342	Tailors, Dressmakers, Furriers and Milliners
4142	Teachers - Elementary School and Kindergarten
4141	Teachers - Secondary School
6221	Technical Sales Specialists - Wholesale Trade
0131	Telecommunication Carriers Managers
7246	Telecommunications Installation and Repair Workers
7245	Telecommunications Line and Cable Workers
7317	Textile Machinery Mechanics and Repairers
5243	Theatre, Fashion, Exhibit and Other Creative Designers
3144	Therapy and Assessment (Other Professional Occupations)
3235	Therapy and Assessment (other Technical Occupations)
7283	Tilesetters
7232	Tool and Die Makers
7383	Trades and Related Occupations (other)
5125	Translators, Terminologists and Interpreters
0713	Transportation Managers
Code	**U**
8231	Underground Production and Development Miners
7341	Upholsterers
2153	Urban and Land Use Planners
2282	User Support Technicians
0912	Utilities Managers
Code	**V**
3114	Veterinarians

3213	Veterinary and Animal Health Technologists and
Code	**W**
7373	Water Well Drillers
2175	Web Designers and Developers
7265	Welders and Related Machine Operators

CITIZENSHIP & IMMIGRATION CANADA

Business Class

Business Class Categories

Canada has three classes of business immigrants: **investors, entrepreneurs** and **self-employed persons**. You must choose to apply under only **one** of these classes, even if you meet the requirements for more than one class. Features of each type are listed below to help you make that decision. Note that you cannot change the class you are applying under once you have submitted your application.

Investors

Investors must have business experience. They must have **either**

> (a) managed a qualifying business and controlled a percentage of equity of a qualifying business for **at least 2 years** in the period beginning 5 years before the date of application, **or**

> (b) they must have managed at least 5 full-time job equivalents per year in a business for **at least 2 years** in the period beginning 5 years before the date of application.

The investor class applicant must have a net worth of at least $800,000. They are required to make an investment of $400,000, paid to the Receiver General of Canada. The investment is subsequently allocated to participating provinces and territories in Canada. These governments use the funds for job creation and economic development. The full amount of the investment (without interest) is repaid to the investor after 5 years. The exact date of repayment depends on when the $400,000 is received by Citizenship and Immigration Canada. At the latest, the amount would be returned 5 years and 3 months after the date of payment. The return of the investment is fully guaranteed by participating provinces and territories.

Features of the Investor Program

> • Investors are not required to start a business in Canada;

> • Investments are fully guaranteed by provinces and territories that participate in the program;

> • The provinces and territories control the investment during the 5 year lock-in period; and

> • No immigration conditions are imposed upon admission to Canada.

Under the *Canada-Quebec Accord*, the province of Quebec operates its own immigrant investor program. All investors in the Quebec program must intend to live in Quebec and must be selected by Quebec. In common with the federal program, investors in the Quebec program must invest $400,000 and have a net worth of $800,000.

Entrepreneurs

Entrepreneurs must have business experience. They must have managed a qualifying business and controlled a percentage of equity of a qualifying business for **at least 2 years** in the period beginning 5 years before the date of application.

The entrepreneur class applicant must have a net worth of at least $300,000. Additionally, they must have the intention and the ability to:

1. Control a percentage of equity of a qualifying Canadian business equal to or greater than 331/3%;

2. Provide active and ongoing management of the qualifying Canadian business; and

3. Create at least one incremental full-time job equivalent for one or more Canadian citizens or permanent residents other than the entrepreneur applicant and their family members.

Entrepreneurs are required to sign a statement that they intend and will be able to meet the conditions or permanent residence.

Features of the Entrepreneur Program

• A minimum net worth requirement of $300,000;

• A requirement that within three years of becoming a permanent resident, the entrepreneur must have controlled and have actively managed a qualifying Canadian business for a period of at least one year, and that the business must have created employment opportunities for others; and

• All family members are admitted under the same conditions as the principal applicant; the conditions are removed once the entrepreneur satisfies the conditions.

Under the *Canada-Quebec Accord*, the province of Quebec operates its own immigrant entrepreneur program. All entrepreneurs in the Quebec program must intend to live in Quebec and must be selected by Quebec. In common with the federal programs, entrepreneurs in the Quebec program must have a net worth of $300,000.

Self-employed persons

Self-employed immigrants must have **relevant experience (see Definitions)**. Points are awarded for relevant experience within the 5 year period immediately preceding the date of application.

Features of the Self-employed persons program

• No immigration conditions are imposed on this class.

• Self-employed immigrants must have the experience, intention and ability to:

· establish a business that will, at a minimum, create an employment opportunity for themselves and that will make a significant contribution to cultural activities or athletics in Canada; or

· purchase and manage a farm in Canada.

CITIZENSHIP & IMMIGRATION CANADA

Point Grid – Business Class

AGE	Maximum 10
21 - 44 years of age at time of application	10
Less 2 points for each year of age over 44 years or under 21 years	

EDUCATION	Maximum 25
You have obtained a Master's or PhD and completed at least 17 years of fulltime or full-time equivalent studies.	25
You have obtained two or more university educational credentials at the bachelor's level and completed at least 15 years of full-time or full-time equivalent studies.	22
You have obtained a three-year post-secondary educational credential and completed at least 15 years of full-time or full-time equivalent studies.	22
You have obtained a two-year educational credential at the bachelor's level and completed at least 14 years of full-time or full-time equivalent studies.	20
You have obtained a two-year post-secondary educational credential and completed at least 14 years of full-time or full-time equivalent studies.	20
You have obtained a one-year university credential at the bachelor's level and completed at least 13 years of full-time or full-time equivalent studies.	15
You have obtained a one-year post-secondary educational credential and completed at least 13 years of full-time or full-time equivalent studies	15
You have obtained a one-year post-secondary educational credential and completed at least 12 years of full-time of full-time equivalent studies.	12
You have obtained a secondary school credential	5
You have not completed secondary school (also called high school)	0

OFFICIAL LANGUAGES *	Maximum 24
Highly functional in first official language	16
Moderately functional in first official language	8
Basically functional or no abilities in first official language	0
Highly functional in second official language	4
Moderately functional in second official language	0
Basically functional or no abilities in second official language	0

BUSINESS EXPERIENCE	Maximum 35
Two years business experience	20
Three years business experience	25
Four years business experience	30
Five years business experience	35
*Business Experience: within five years preceding date of application	

ADAPTABILITY	Maximum 6
Your accompanying spouse or common-law partner's level of education	
Secondary school (high school) diploma or less	0
A one or two-year post-secondary educational credential **and** at least 13 years of education	3
A three-year post secondary educational credential **and** at least 15 years of education	4
A three-year university credential **and** at least 15 years of education	4
A Master's or PhD **and** at least 17 years of education	5
You or your accompanying spouse or common-law partner has studied in Canada	
Obtained a Canadian post-secondary educational credential of at least two years since the age of 18	5
You or your accompanying spouse or common-law partner has worked in Canada	
Worked full-time in Canada for at least one year	5
You or your accompanying spouse or common-law partner has family in Canada	
Have a parent, grandparent, aunt, uncle, sister, brother, nephew, niece, child or grandchild who is a Canadian citizen or permanent resident living in Canada	5

TOTAL	Maximum 100
PASS MARKS FOR ALL THE THREE CLASSES	35

N.B. This selection grid and point system does not apply to persons who are selected under the Quebec Program. Under the terms of the Canada-Quebec Accord, Quebec selects its own business immigrants.

CITIZENSHIP & IMMIGRATION CANADA

Selection Procedure

You must first meet the definition of the one class you are applying under (investor, entrepreneur or self-employed person) to be eligible for selection. If you successfully meet the definition, you are then assessed against 5 selection factors: age, education, official languages, experience and adaptability. For each selection factor, a specific number of selection points are allotted. The following tables will help you estimate how many points you would earn for each factor. It is important that you make a careful assessment before you apply because you must pay certain fees, one of which is non-refundable (the Processing fee) even if your application is refused. If you have a score lower than a total of 35 points, your application may be refused. The pass mark for all three classes of business immigrants is 35.

Investors and Entrepreneurs

Factor 1: Business experience (maximum 35 points)

Business experience must have been obtained within the period beginning 5 years before the date of application.

Two years business experience	20
Three years business experience	25
Four years business experience	30
Five years business experience	35

Factor 2: Age (maximum 10 points)

Points are given for your age at the time your application is received.

Age	Total Points
16 or under	0
17	2
18	4
19	6
20	8
21 - 49	10
50	8
51	6
52	4
53	2
54 and over	0

Factor 3: Education (maximum 25 points)

You have not completed secondary school (also called high school)	0
You have obtained a secondary school credential	5
You have obtained a 1-year post-secondary educational credential and completed at least 12 years of full-time or full-time equivalent studies.	12
You have obtained a 1-year post-secondary educational credential and completed at least 13 years of full-time or full-time equivalent studies	15
You have obtained a 1-year university credential at the bachelor's level and completed at least 13 years of full-time or full-time equivalent studies.	15
You have obtained a 2-year post-secondary educational credential and completed at least 14 years of full-time or full-time equivalent studies.	20
You have obtained a 2-year educational credential at the bachelor's level and completed at least 14 years of full-time or full-time equivalent studies.	20
You have obtained a three-year post-secondary educational credential and completed at least 15 years of full-time or full-time equivalent studies.	22
You have obtained 2 or more university educational credentials at the bachelor's level and completed at least 15 years of full-time or full-time equivalent studies.	**22**
You have obtained a Master's or PhD and completed at least 17 years of fulltime or full-time equivalent studies.	**25**

Factor 4: English and French language ability (maximum 24 points)

To assess your English and French language ability, first decide which language you are most comfortable with. This language is your **first official language.** The language you feel less comfortable communicating with is your **second official language.** Next, award points according to your ability to read, write, listen to and speak English and French. The following two tables define the levels of language proficiency and how points are allotted for each level:

Skill Level	Criteria
High proficiency	You can communicate effectively in most community and workplace situations. You speak, listen to, read and write the language very well.
Moderate proficiency	You can make yourself understood and you understand what others are saying in most workplace and community situations. You speak, listen to, read and write the language well.
Basic proficiency	You do not meet the above criteria for moderate proficiency but still have some ability to speak, listen to, read or write the language.
No proficiency	You have no ability whatsoever in speaking, listening to, reading or writing the language.

Calculating your language points

First official language	Read	Write	Listen	Speak	Maximum score per category
High proficiency	4	4	4	4	16
Moderate proficiency	2	2	2	2	8
Basic proficiency	1	1	1	1	2
No proficiency	0	0	0	0	0
Maximum possible score for all 4 abilities in first official language =					16

Second official language	Read	Write	Listen	Speak	Maximum score per category
High proficiency	2	2	2	2	8
Moderate proficiency	2	2	2	2	8
Basic proficiency	1	1	1	1	2
No proficiency	0	0	0	0	0
Maximum possible score for all 4 abilities in second official language =					8
Maximum possible score total for both official languages =					24

Factor 5: Adaptability (maximum 6 points)

A maximum of 6 points for adaptability can be earned by any combination of the following elements:

You have made a business exploration trip to Canada in the period beginning 5 years before the date of application.	6
You have participated in joint federal-provincial business immigration initiatives.	6

Self-employed Persons

Factor 1: Relevant experience (maximum 35 points)

Experience must have been obtained within the 5 year period immediately preceding the date of application.

Two years relevant experience	20
Three years relevant experience	25
Four years relevant experience	30
Five years relevant experience	35

Factor 2: Age (maximum 10 points)

Points are given for your age at the time your application is received.

Age	Total Points
16 or under	0
17	2
18	4
19	6
20	8
21 - 49	10
50	8
51	6
52	4
53	2
54 and over	0

Factor 3: Education (maximum 25 points)

You have not completed secondary school (also called high school)	0
You have obtained a secondary school credential	5
You have obtained a 1-year post-secondary educational credential and completed at least 12 years of full-time or full-time equivalent studies.	12
You have obtained a 1-year post-secondary educational credential and completed at least 13 years of full-time or full-time equivalent studies	15
You have obtained a 1-year university credential at the bachelor's level and completed at least 13 years of full-time or full-time equivalent studies.	15
You have obtained a 2-year post-secondary educational credential and completed at least 14 years of full-time or full-time equivalent studies.	20
You have obtained a 2-year educational credential at the bachelor's level and completed at least 14 years of full-time or full-time equivalent studies.	20
You have obtained a three-year post-secondary educational credential and completed at least 15 years of full-time or full-time equivalent studies.	22
You have obtained 2 or more university educational credentials at the bachelor's level and completed at least 15 years of full-time or full-time equivalent studies.	22
You have obtained a Master's or PhD and completed at least 17 years of fulltime or full-time equivalent studies.	25

Factor 4: English and French language ability (maximum 24 points)

To assess your English and French language ability, first decide which language you are most comfortable with. This language is your **first official language.** The language you feel less comfortable communicating with is your **second official language.** Next, award points according to your ability to read, write, listen to and speak English and French. The following two tables define the levels of language proficiency and how points are allotted for each level:

Skill Level	Criteria
High proficiency	You can communicate effectively in most community and workplace situations. You speak, listen, read and write the language very well.
Moderate proficiency	You can make yourself understood and you understand what others are saying in most workplace and community situations. You speak, listen, read and write the language well.
Basic proficiency	You do not meet the above criteria for moderate proficiency but still have some ability to speak, listen to, read or write the language.
No proficiency	You have no ability whatsoever in speaking, listening to, reading or writing the language.

Calculating your language points

First official language	Read	Write	Listen	Speak	Maximum score per category
High proficiency	4	4	4	4	16
Moderate proficiency	2	2	2	2	8
Basic proficiency	1	1	1	1	2
No proficiency	0	0	0	0	0
Maximum possible score for all 4 abilities in first official language =					16

Second official language	Read	Write	Listen	Speak	Maximum score per category
High proficiency	2	2	2	2	8
Moderate proficiency	2	2	2	2	8
Basic proficiency	1	1	1	1	2
No proficiency	0	0	0	0	0
Maximum possible score for all 4 abilities in second official language =					8
Maximum possible score total for both official languages =					24

Factor 5: Adaptability (maximum 6 points)

A maximum of 6 points for adaptability can be earned by any combination of the following elements:

1	**Your accompanying spouse or common-law partner's level of education**	
	Secondary school (high school) diploma or less	0
	A 1 or 2-year post-secondary educational credential and at least 13 years of education	3
A three-year post secondary educational credential and at least 15 years of education	4	
	A three-year university credential and at least 15 years of education	4
	A Master's or PhD and at least 17 years of education	5
2	**You or your accompanying spouse or common-law partner has studied in Canada**	
	Not at all, or anything less than 2 years post-secondary education in Canada	0
	Obtained a Canadian post-secondary educational credential of at least 2 years since the age of 18	5
3	**You or your accompanying spouse or common-law partner has worked in Canada**	
	Not at all, or less than 1 year full-time work in Canada	0
Worked full-time in Canada for at least 1 year	5	
4	**You or your accompanying spouse or common-law partner has family in Canada**	
	No	0
	Have a parent, grandparent, aunt, uncle, sister, brother, nephew, niece, child or grandchild who is a Canadian citizen or permanent resident living in Canada	5

CITIZENSHIP & IMMIGRATION CANADA

Document Check List

Assemble all your documents as listed. Check (x) each applicable item on the checklist and attach the checklist to your documents (a paper clip will do). Place all the documents in a sealed envelope.

Do not send originals. Send photocopies of all documents, **except** the *Certificat de sélection du Québec (CSQ)*, if your intention is to reside in the province of Québec, and the police certificates, which must be **originals**. If your documents are not in English or French, send a notarized (certified) translation with a copy of the originals.

If you are unable to provide any of the requested documentation for special reasons, please attach a **written explanation** with full details as to why that documentation is unavailable.

1 APPLICATION FORM

Check that it is completed, signed and dated. Your signed application should include:

1. *Application for Permanent Residence in Canada* with a stapled envelope containing photos.

2. *Schedule 1 - Background / Declaration* completed and signed by you and each of your family members 18 years or older.

3. *Schedule 6 - Economic Classes - Business Immigrants* completed and signed by you.

4. *Additional Family Information* completed by you, your spouse or common-law partner and each dependent child aged 18 or over (whether accompanying you or not).

If you want us to deal with a Canadian representative on your behalf, be sure you have completed and signed the *Authority to Release Information to Designated Individuals* form. Include in the same envelope the completed application forms.

2 IDENTITY AND CIVIL STATUS DOCUMENTS

Birth, marriage, final divorce, annulment or separation certificates for you and spouse; death certificate for former spouse if applicable.

3 CHILDREN'S INFORMATION

Children's birth certificates (which name their parents); adoption papers for adopted dependent children; proof of custody for children under the age of 22 and proof that the children may be removed from the jurisdiction of the court; if the children will not accompany you to Canada, proof that you have fulfilled any obligation stated in custody agreements. Statutory declaration that the remaining father or mother has no objection to the child living in Canada.

4 POLICE CERTIFICATES AND CLEARANCES

Police certificates or clearances from each country in which you and everyone in your family aged 18 years or over have resided six months or more since reaching 18 years of age. **You must attach the original police document(s).** If these certificates are in a language other than English or French, they must be accompanied by a certified translation in either English or French.

5 BACKGROUND DOCUMENTS (if applicable)

Any document to support your answers to questions in the *Background/Declaration* form such as completion of military service card, military records, membership cards or any documents showing your association or involvement in any social, political, vocational and cultural organization.

6 TRAVEL DOCUMENTS AND PASSPORTS

Passports or travel documents for yourself, your spouse and dependent children. Include only copies of pages showing the passport number, date of issue and expiration, your photo, name, date and place of birth. If you live in a country other than your country of nationality, include a copy of your visa for the country in which you currently live.

7 SETTLEMENT FUNDS

You must provide proof of sufficient funds currently available to maintain yourself and your family members until you are self-supporting in Canada. These funds must be readily transferable to Canada in a convertible currency. Financial statements for the last three (3) years (bank accounts, shares certificates, portfolio, etc.). Proof of assets (properties, buildings, lands, etc.).

Note: If you carry more than $10,000 Canadian in cash funds upon your entry to Canada, you will have to disclose these funds to a Canadian official upon arrival. Cash funds means money (coins or bank notes), securities in bearer form (stocks, bonds, debentures, treasury bills etc.) and negotiable instruments in bearer form (bankers drafts, cheques, travellers' cheques, money orders etc.). Failure to disclose can result in fines and imprisonment.

8 FEE PAYMENT

Contact the visa office to which you will be applying **before** submitting your application to find out the acceptable method for paying the fees. **Do not enclose cash.** You must submit the acceptable fee payment **with** your completed application.

9 CERTIFICAT DE SÉLECTION DU QUÉBEC (CSQ)

Original of the *Certificat de sélection du Québec (CSQ)* if your intention is to reside in the province of Québec.

10 ADDITIONAL INFORMATION

Any document or record to demonstrate your adaptability, initiative, motivation, or resourcefulness. All school certificates, diplomas and degrees for you and your spouse or common-law partner (if applicable), including apprenticeship or trade papers. Letters of reference or work certificates from present and past employers for you and your spouse or common-law partner.

There are Business Immigration Centres (BICs) specially staffed to assess potential business immigrants. You may wish to consider mailing your application directly to a BIC to obtain a more specialized processing of your application.

You must contact the BIC before you mail your application to find out the acceptable methods for paying the fees. The acceptable fee payment must accompany your application.

CITIZENSHIP & IMMIGRATION CANADA

Important Definition

Accompanying dependant: A spouse, common-law partner or dependent child of the principal applicant who intends to obtain permanent resident status in Canada. Accompanying dependants can travel separately from the principal applicant but must not arrive in Canada before the principal applicant.

Business experience:

- In respect to an **investor,** means:

  · The management of a **qualifying business** and the control of a **percentage of equity** of a qualifying business for at least 2 years in the period beginning five years before the date of application; or

  · The management of at least 5 **full-time job equivalents** per year in a business for at least 2 years in the period beginning 5 years before the date of application.

- In respect to an **entrepreneur**, means:

  · The management of a **qualifying business** and the control of a **percentage of equity** of a qualifying business for at least 2 years in the period beginning five years before the date of application.

***Certificat de sélection du Quebec* (CSQ):** A document issued by the Ministère des Relations avec les citoyens et de l'Immigration (MRCI), indicating that an immigration candidate has been accepted to live in the province of Quebec upon arrival in Canada.

Common-law partner: A person who is living in a conjugal relationship with another person, either of the same or opposite sex, who has done so for a period of at least 1 year.

Dependent children: Daughters and sons, including children adopted before the age of 18, who:

- are under the age of 22 and not a spouse or common-law partner; or

- have been continuously enrolled and in attendance as full-time students in an educational institution and financially supported by their parents since turning 22 (or from the date of becoming a spouse or common-law partner if this happened before the age of 22); or

- depend substantially on the financial support of their parents since turning 22 and are unable to support themselves due to a medical condition.

Educational credential: Any diploma, degree, trade or apprenticeship credential issued for the completion of a program of study or training at a recognized educational or training institution.

Family member: A spouse, common-law partner, dependent child, or dependent child of a dependent child of the principal applicant. The spouse or common-law partner of the principal applicant's dependent child is also considered a family member.

Full-time equivalent studies: With respect to part-time or accelerated studies, the period that would have been required to complete those studies on a full-time basis.

Full-time job equivalent: Defined as 1,950 hours of paid employment.

Net assets: Assets minus liabilities plus shareholder loans from the applicant and their spouse or common-law partner.

Net income: After tax profit or loss plus remuneration to the applicant and their spouse or common-law partner.

Net worth: The fair market value of the assets of the applicant and their spouse or common-law partner minus the fair market value of all their liabilities.

Percentage of equity:

• In respect of a sole proprietorship, 100% of the equity of a sole proprietorship.

• In respect of a corporation, the percentage of the issued and outstanding voting shares of the capital stock of the corporation controlled by the applicant or their spouse or common-law partner.

• In respect of a partnership or joint venture, the percentage of the profit or loss of a partnership or joint venture to which the applicant or their spouse or common-law partner is entitled.

Post-secondary credential: Any diploma, certificate, or other credential other than a university credential issued for the completion of a program of study or training at a recognized educational or training institution.

Qualifying business: A business—other than a business operated primarily for the purpose of deriving investment income such as interest, dividends or capital gains—for which, in each of any 2 years in the period beginning 5 years before the date of application and ending on the date of the interview decision, there is proof of any 2 of the following:

1. That the percentage of equity multiplied by the number of full-time job equivalents is equal to or greater than 2 full-time job equivalents per year;

2. That the percentage of equity multiplied by the total annual sales is equal to or greater than $500,000;

3. That the percentage of equity multiplied by the net income in the year is equal to or greater than $50,000; and

4. That the percentage of equity multiplied by the net assets at the end of the year is equal to or greater than $125,000.

Qualifying Canadian business: A business operated in Canada by an entrepreneur—other than a business operated primarily for the purpose of deriving investment income, such as interest, dividends or capital gains—for which there is, in any year within the period of three years after the day the entrepreneur becomes a permanent resident, evidence of any 2 of the following:

1. That the percentage of equity multiplied by the number of full-time job equivalents is equal to or greater than 2 full-time job equivalents per year;

2. That the percentage of equity multiplied by the total annual sales is equal to or greater than $250,000;

3. That the percentage of equity multiplied by the net income in the year is equal to or greater than $25,000; and

4. That the percentage of equity multiplied by the net assets at the end of the year is equal to or greater than $125,000.

Relevant experience: In respect to a **self-employed person**, means

• For at least 2 years in the period beginning 5 years before the date of application:

· Self-employment in cultural activities or athletics; or

· Participation, at the world-class level, in cultural activities or athletics; or

· Farm management experience.

Spouse: A person of the opposite sex who is 16 years of age or older and to whom the applicant is legally married.

Visa office: A Canadian immigration office outside Canada, located at a Canadian Embassy, High Commission or Consulate.

CITIZENSHIP & IMMIGRATION CANADA

Federal - Provincial Agreements

Under the Constitution, immigration is shared between the federal government and the provinces, with federal legislation prevailing. The **Immigration Act** (Section 108) allows the Minister to enter into agreements with the provinces to facilitate the co-ordination and implementation of immigration policies and programs.

Since 1978, seven provinces have signed immigration agreements (British Columbia and Ontario have yet to do so). Discussions are under way with several provinces toward new or revised immigration agreements or other types of working arrangements.

These federal-provincial agreements outline specific responsibilities and establish formal mechanisms by which the provinces can contribute to the development of immigration policies and programs.

The **Canada-Quebec Accord**, the most comprehensive agreement to date, was signed in February 1991. It gives Quebec sole responsibility for selecting independent immigrants and refugees abroad who are destined for Quebec. It also allows Quebec to provide its own reception and integration services -- linguistic, cultural and economic -- for permanent residents of the province. Federally, Canada maintains responsibility for defining general immigrant categories, setting levels for admitting persons to Canada and enforcement.

Other mechanisms are also in place to facilitate federal-provincial co-operation. Federal, provincial and territorial deputy ministers responsible for immigration meet on a regular basis. As a result of these meetings, federal-provincial working groups have been formed to examine specific immigration issues. These include access to professions and trades, sponsorship, business immigration, promotion and recruitment, settlement and language training, and information sharing and research.

THE *CANADA-QUEBEC ACCORD*

Due to Quebec's responsibilities in immigration, as defined in the **Canada-Quebec Accord**, persons destined for this province may have to meet different requirements.

VISITORS, STUDENTS AND FOREIGN WORKERS

People coming to Quebec to study, receive medical treatment or work in a position requiring a job validation (a condition that no Canadian is available to perform the work) must first obtain the province's consent.

SELECTION

The *Accord* specifically gives Quebec exclusive responsibility for selecting all independent immigrants and refugees abroad who are destined for Quebec. Those selected by the province will receive a document called *Certificat de sélection de Québec* (CSQ). The federal government ensures that statutory admission requirements, such as medical and criminal checks, are met before issuing a visa.

For the Family Class category, *Le ministère des Relations avec les citoyens et de l'Immigration* (MRCI), *Direction de l'aide à l'immigration d'affaires* assesses if sponsors are financially able to meet sponsorship obligations and, once approved, notifies the appropriate visa office.

FEES

The Quebec government has set fees for some of the immigration-related services provided by MRCI. People seeking information on current fees should contact MRCI directly.

SETTLEMENT RESPONSIBILITIES

The province provides reception and integration services to new permanent residents of Quebec. These services must be equivalent to those provided by the federal government elsewhere in the country.

CITIZENSHIP AND IMMIGRATION CANADA

British Columbia Nominee Program

An Introduction

The British Columbia Provincial Nominee Program (BC PNP) has been developed to assist employers fill critical skill shortages. The BC PNP is a special component of the Canadian immigration program. Nomination through the BC PNP removes the requirement to meet the occupation points screen and allows for faster processing. Under the BC PNP immigration processing will take approximately six months, rather than the eighteen months to two years that it otherwise does. The temporary foreign worker program is currently used to meet some critical skill shortages but this is a temporary solution for employer and employee. In contrast, use of the BC PNP to meet critical skill shortages adds to the permanent workforce.

The BC PNP is employer-driven. An employer has a permanent, full-time vacancy in a field where there is a shortage of qualified workers. The employer recruits a qualified person, and then applies for nomination for that person.

A further goal of the BC PNP is increasing economic benefit to the provincial economy. The BC PNP is aimed at high skilled occupations, where the potential for gains to the economy are substantial and where it is expected that there will be a transfer of skills to the BC workforce. These occupations typically require considerable education. Other positions might be skilled trades where the lack of qualified workers is causing a bottleneck to production. The BC PNP will also be complementary to education and training policies. Skill shortages that can be met by BC training programs (short-term training) will not be appropriate for PNP use.

The BC PNP views employers as partners. This is a central principle of the program. It is assumed that employers use international recruiting (which is costly and time-consuming) only for very good reasons. Therefore, requests for nomination from employers will be viewed as valid, unless inconsistent employer and job information raises concerns. It is understood that any immigration program could be open to inappropriate applications, but it is expected that these will be screened out in the assessment process.

The BC PNP is not run by a specific skill shortage list. Rather, the BC PNP has identified certain sectors as high priorities and has drawn together information on well-documented shortages. The initial priorities include high technology workers and certain highly skilled trades. Despite current communications and Internet business weaknesses, the IT sector is seen as a priority, especially in software development. Another priority is recruiting technicians for the aerospace sector. Post- secondary education is also being considered, because of anticipated large numbers of retirements and because the current practice of preferentially hiring Canadians, sometimes impedes obtaining the best person. Other areas, such as skilled trades, small to medium sized employers, and employers facing geographic impacts, may also be addressed.

These priorities are not exhaustive. Employers in other industries who identify key shortages and the need to recruit from outside of Canada are welcome to apply to the BC PNP. These priorities are open to addition and change as additional information on skill shortages develop.

The BC PNP will ensure program integrity through assessment of information on shortages, companies, job descriptions (including pay & working conditions) and qualifications of potential nominees. The Employer Kit outlines the full requirements for the BC PNP process. The BC PNP is aware of the need to minimise the workload for employers so employers are encouraged to make contact early on; if the vacancy and worker are in skills which have already been identified as being in shortage, some documentation requirements may be waived.

This assessment process calls on the BC PNP officers to exercise discretion and there is a need for sound information. Employer associations and employers are seen as crucial in providing current information on shortages, especially on emerging skills. The BC PNP wishes to share information with
employers so that they will also self-screen and submit nominations that are consistent with the program objective of meeting critical shortages in high skill occupations.

BC PNP
http://www.pnp.mi.gov.bc.ca

Application Procedure

Applications will be accepted in three categories:

1. Strategic Occupations

To qualify under the strategic occupations category, a prospective nominee must:

- Have a guaranteed job offer from an employer in British Columbia, in an occupation experiencing a critical labour market shortage;

- Confirm the eligibility of a publicly funded occupation prior to applying to the BC PNP. Please contact the BC PNP office regarding the eligibility of a publicly funded job offer, only certain occupations are eligible;

- Not be a business owner. A prospective nominee will only be considered an employee if the percentage of ownership in the company is less than 50%

- Have valid immigration status if living in or visiting Canada. Without valid immigration status, a prospective nominee is in violation of the federal *Immigration and Refugee Protection Act.*

- Overview of the BC PNP

- BC PNP private sector priorities.

- Health Match BC - Foreign trained nurses wishing to learn more about job opportunities in B.C.

For more information on the Strategic Occupations category of the BC PNP, contact:

B.C. Ministry of Community, Aboriginal and Woman's Services (Immigration Branch)
PO Box 9214 Stn. Prov. Gov't
Victoria, BC, V8W 9J1
Phone: 250-387-6540
Fax: 250-387-3725
Email: PNPinfo@Victoria1.gov.bc.ca

2. Business Skills (Currently under development)

- For individuals with specific business projects who have proven abilities and financial resources to establish a business in B.C. For program information on the Business components, please contact:

General Inquiries
Ministry of Competition, Science and Enterprise
BC Trade and Investment Office
999 Canada Place Vancouver, BC V6C 3E1
Phone: (604) 844-1815
Email: Bus.imm@gems7.gov.bc.ca

3. Projects (Currently under development)

- For program information on the Project components please contact:

General Inquiries
Ministry of Competition, Science and Enterprise
BC Trade and Investment Office
999 Canada Place Vancouver, BC V6C 3E1
Phone: (604) 844-1815
Email: Bus.imm@gems7.gov.bc.ca

BC PNP
http://www.pnp.mi.gov.bc.ca

Frequently Asked Questions

1. How much faster is immigration under the BC PNP, compared to other Canadian immigration programs?

Times will vary from case to case, depending on individual circumstances. However, immigration under the BC PNP is significantly faster, compared to other Canadian immigration programs.

2. Will it speed up the process if I apply to the BC PNP and to Citizenship and Immigration Canada at the same time?

No. In fact, it would cause confusion and actually slow the process down.

If you have already applied to Citizenship and Immigration Canada, British Columbia will still consider your provincial nominee application. However, the application process may be slower.

3. What if I apply to another province's Provincial Nominee Program? Will that speed up my B.C. application?

No. B.C. is looking for a solid commitment from you to live and work in British Columbia. If you apply to another province at the same time, it could suggest that you are not serious about wanting to come to B.C.

4. What is the Canadian government's role in the BC PNP?

The Canadian government conducts medical and security checks and issues visas for people who immigrate under the BC PNP.

5. If I am approved for the BC PNP, does that guarantee my immigration to Canada?

No. The BC PNP only allows British Columbia to nominate people for immigration. Successful nominees must still meet Canadian medical and security requirements for immigration.

6. What about my family? Does the BC PNP allow them to immigrate with me?

Yes. An individual's spouse and dependents may accompany a nominee under the BC PNP.

7. What if I already live in British Columbia? Can I use the BC PNP to help my family members immigrate?

If your family members meet the criteria for the BC PNP, they are eligible to apply. However, the BC PNP is a targeted economic program, designed for a limited number of individuals.

BC PNP
http://www.pnp.mi.gov.bc.ca

Manitoba Nominee Program

Business Program

The Province of Manitoba and Government of Canada share responsibilities regarding business people immigrating to Canada through the Manitoba Provincial Nominee Immigration Program for Business.

The Manitoba Provincial Nominee Immigration Program for business allows Manitoba to recruit, select, and nominate qualified business people from around the world who have the intent and ability to move to Manitoba and establish or purchase a business.

To qualify for the program, applicants must meet the following criteria:

- minimum personal networth of CDN $250,000;

- minimum amount of equity investment in Manitoba of CDN $150,000;

- demonstrated business experience or extensive experience in senior management of a successful company;

- conducted a visit or planning a visit to Manitoba within few months of applying to explore business opportunities and Manitoba's quality of life; and

- must supply a Letter of Credit from a recognized financial institution to the Government of Manitoba, in the amount of CDN $75,000 guaranteeing the establishment or purchase of a business in Manitoba. The Letter of Credit will be released when the investment is made and the intended business is undertaken as outlined in the application.

Manitoba would like to accept all applicants who meet the program criteria for nomination, however our agreement with the Government of Canada limits the number of immigrants that we may nominate each year. Given this limitation, Manitoba will select the applicants who best meet the qualifications and who offer the most to Manitoba.

Applicants who are nominated by the Province of Manitoba will be required to apply for immigrant visa through a Canadian Visa Office. If you are accepted for nomination, assistance will be provided in preparing an application to a Canada Visa Office for permanent resident visa for you and your dependents.

BUSINESS EXPLORATORY VISIT TO MANITOBA:

We appreciate your interest in the Province of Manitoba, Canada. As you are spending your valuable time and money on an exploratory visit to our Province, we want to ensure that you maximize the benefit you derive from your time here. For this reason we require the following information at least two weeks (or more) prior to your planned visit to Manitoba:

- A detailed résumé listing all of your training and education, work history and business activities. Please ensure you provide details on any business(es) you have started as well as on your managerial experience, specifically the various roles and responsibilities that you assumed;

- Copies of the latest financial statements for your business, or for the company for which you work;

- Statement of your personal net worth detailing your assets, liabilities and net worth (sample template attached);

- An indication of the amount of money you intend to transfer to Manitoba for establishing or purchasing a business and for settlement; and

- An indication of the type of business, or businesses, you wish to explore while in Manitoba.

Having this information in advance will help us prepare for your visit and allow you to maximize the benefit you derive from your time here. All of your personal financial information will remain confidential. It will be used to ensure that you meet basic requirements and to identify potential opportunities that match your capabilities and interests.

If you would like to make an exploratory visit to Manitoba, please send the above documents, along with your full mailing address, telephone number, fax number e-mail address and an indication of when you would like to make your visit, to the following address:

Business Immigration Office,
Manitoba Trade and Investment Corporation
410-155 Carlton Street, Winnipeg, Manitoba Canada R3C 3H8
Tele: (204) 945-1819 / Fax: (204) 948-2179
Toll Free In Canada and U.S.: 1-800-529-9981
mailto:pnp-b@gov.mb.ca

MB PNP
http://www.gov.mb.ca

Documents Checklist

1. IMMIGRANT APPLICATION FORM (IMM 0008)

Completed and signed form IMM 0008 from each family member over the age of 18, whether they are accompanying you to Canada or not. Photocopy of one current passport-size photograph for each member of your family. Do not send originals. Original photographs will be needed for CIC later. Previous refusal letter(s) or other correspondence from CIC and/or Provincial Nominee programs.
Attach additional pages, where necessary. Write form number on the top of each additional page.

2. ADDITIONAL FAMILY INFORMATION (IMM 5406)

Completed and signed form IMM 5406 from each family member over the age of 18, whether they are accompanying you to Canada or not.

3. MANITOBA SUPPLEMENTARY INFORMATION FORM (MBSUP)

Only ONE MBSUP form to be completed. Check that the appropriate questions are answered in full by the principal applicant and the form is signed by both principal applicant and spouse, if married. Spouse must sign even if not accompanying you to Canada.

Note: Do not leave Personal Net Worth blank. If you do not have funds or own property, indicate how you will obtain necessary settlement funds.

4. INFORMATION RELEASE FORM (MBREL)

Completed, signed by principal applicant and spouse, dated and witnessed. A witness can be any person, including a friend or family member, and need not be a lawyer or notary.

5. RELEASE OF INFORMATION FOR EVALUATION OF PNP (MBEVA)

Completed, signed by principal applicant and spouse, dated and witnessed. A witness can be any person including a friend, or family member, and need not be a lawyer or notary.

6. IDENTITY / MARRIAGE INFORMATION

Birth certificates, for both you and your spouse, showing names of parents. If applicable, also provide:

Marriage certificate

Death certificate

Divorce certificate or proof of separation

National Identity Card/Certificate or Cedula
(If the information differs on any of these documents, provide a sworn affidavit explaining the differences.)

If divorced or separated and you have children under the age of 18 provide:

- Custody agreement for children under the age of 18.

• If children are accompanying you, provide proof that they may do so. This could include a letter from former spouse supporting your move.

• If children are not accompanying you, prove that you have fulfilled any obligations stated in custody agreement. This could include a letter from spouse giving permission for PA to move from the country.

7. CHILDREN'S INFORMATION

Birth certificate for each child showing parentage (naming both parents).

Adoption papers

If dependent children are over 19 years of age, submit proof of continuous full time studies. Provide letter(s) from the school(s), signed by a school official, confirming continued enrolment in full time studies since turning 19 years of age.

8. PASSPORT / TRAVEL DOCUMENTS

Copies of passport or travel documents that are valid for at least two years for yourself, your spouse and dependent children. Submit copies of pages showing the passport number, date of issue and expiration, your photo, name, date and place of birth, as well as occupation, if applicable.

If you live in a country other than your country of citizenship, include a copy of your visa for the country in which you currently live.

Include copies of entry visas or Immigration stamps in your passport from previous visits to Canada.

9. EDUCATION INFORMATION

Educational degrees, diplomas or certificates, and professional licences, for both the principal applicant and spouse.

Official transcripts showing school(s) attended, courses taken and duration of program, must also be included.

All documents must be translated into English or French.

10. EVIDENCE OF LANGUAGE ABILITY IN ENGLISH AND/OR FRENCH

Proof of your ability in English or French.

11. EMPLOYMENT INFORMATION

Copies of letters of reference detailing both the principal applicant and spouse's work experience for the past 10 years, including present employment. Each letter must include:

• specific period of employment with the company (start and end dates).

• position(s) held, and time spent in each position.

• list of tasks/duties and main responsibilities in each position.

• letter must be on company letterhead and signed by an authorized representative of the company, including their name and title.

12. EMPLOYMENT OFFER

Offer of employment to include job title, job description and salary.

13. REGIONAL DEVELOPMENT

Proof of your ties to a rural or northern region of Manitoba.

14. PROOF OF RELATIONSHIP TO FAMILY IN MANITOBA

Birth certificates (showing parents' names) of the relatives through whom you
trace your roots AND Relative's Canadian Passport, Certificate of Citizenship, or Record of
Landing (IMM 1000) AND Relative's Manitoba Health Card

15. FAMILY-LIKE SUPPORT

• Affidavit of Family-Like Support signed by five adults (form available from Manitoba
Labour and Immigration), AND

• Canadian Citizenship certificate or Canadian birth certificate or Record of Landing (IMM
1000) for each of the five adults, AND

• Manitoba Health Card for each of the five adults.

16. EVIDENCE OF EDUCATION IN MANITOBA

Student authorization and proof of attendance from education institution.

17. EVIDENCE OF WORK IN MANITOBA

Employment authorization and letter of reference from employer.

18. SETTLEMENT FUNDS

Letters from financial institutions

Bank account statements

Proof of liquid assets

Proof of ownership of real properties (land and buildings) AND an objective price
evaluation

19. TAGS TO ATTACH TO EACH OF THE ABOVE DOCUMENTS

PUT ALL PHOTOCOPIES OF YOUR APPLICATIONS AND DOCUMENTS TOGETHER AND
FORWARD THEM IN A SEALED ENVELOPE TO:

Manitoba Labour and Immigration
Manitoba Provincial Nominee Program
9th Floor – 213 Notre Dame Avenue
Winnipeg, Manitoba, R3B 1N3
CANADA

We do not accept applications received over the Internet, via electronic mail (e-mail) or by fax, as
forms sent in these ways often arrive incomplete, mixed and/or illegible.

Your application will be reviewed and you will be contacted in writing. The program officer may
request other documents to complete the assessment of your application.

You will be told of the decision of the assessment in writing. Final decisions will not be given over the telephone.

If you are accepted for the Manitoba Provincial Nominee program, you will receive a letter and further instructions about how to proceed with your application. You will need the original copy of your forms and supporting documents to comply with the instructions you will receive.

MB PNP
http://www.gov.mb.ca

HIGH DEMAND OCCUPATIONS

MANITOBA PROVINCIAL NOMINEE PROGRAM

Aircraft Assembler & Inspector
Aircraft Maintenance Engineer
Aircraft Maintenance Technician
Bricklayer
Cabinetmaker
Computer Engineer
Computer Programmer
Electrical & Electronic Engineering Technologist and Technician
Electrical & Electronics Engineer
Heavy-duty Equipment Mechanic
Industrial and Manufacturing Engineer
Industrial Engineering and Manufacturing Technologist and Technician
Industrial Instrument Technician
Information Systems Business Analyst and Consultant
Long Haul Truck Driver
Machining Tool Operator
Machinist
Motor Vehicle Body Repairer
Motor Vehicle Mechanic
Nondestructive Tester and Inspector
Pattern maker in Garment Manufacturing
Sheet Metal Worker
Software Engineer
Tool & Die Maker
Web Designer/Graphic Illustrator
Welder

Guaranteed Job Offer from Manitoba Employer required for the Following Occupations:

Chef
College & Other Vocational Instructor
Construction Contractor/Manager
Financial Auditors and Accountant
Hog Barn Manager
Information Systems & Data Processing Manager
Marketing & Advertising Manager; fluent in English or French
Pork Production Technician
Psychologist
Social and Community Services Worker and Family Counsellor
Technical Sales Specialist
University Professor

Frequently Asked Questions

What is the Manitoba Provincial Nominee program (MB PNP)?

The Manitoba Provincial Nominee program is an immigration program. It allows the government of Manitoba to recruit and assess immigrants who are best suited to contribute to the province's economy and who intend to live and work in Manitoba. The MB PNP seeks out potential immigrants who are good candidates for Manitoba but who otherwise may not qualify under Canada's immigration criteria. An applicant nominated by Manitoba should receive favourable and prompt consideration from Citizenship and Immigration Canada as long as they comply with medical and statutory requirements.

There are two categories of immigrants under the Provincial Nominee program. One is skilled workers and the other is business immigrants. This application kit has information and forms for skilled workers; that is, individuals with a combination of education, training and experience that allow them to contribute to and benefit from Manitoba's economic growth. Information on the Manitoba Provincial Nominee program for business is available on the Internet at www.immigratemanitoba.com or by contacting Manitoba Labour and Immigration at (Canada 001) 204-945-2806.

Manitoba Provincial Nominee program for skilled workers

Under the MB PNP for skilled workers, Manitoba recruits, screens and nominates prospective immigrants with the skills to fill specific Manitoba labour market requirements. If you are a skilled worker and are interested in living and working in Manitoba, you have the best chance of being nominated if:

- your training and work experience is in demand in Manitoba;

- you have a guaranteed job offer consistent with your training and experience; and

- you have settlement supports in Manitoba to assist you upon your arrival in Manitoba.

The above factors are determined when your application is assessed according to the criteria outlined in this kit. If Manitoba nominates you, a Certificate of Nomination will be issued. You can then apply for a permanent resident visa through Citizenship and Immigration Canada (CIC). You must still meet the federal regulatory requirements (medical examination, security and criminal checks) as outlined by CIC.

How do I know if I should apply for the Manitoba Provincial Nominee program?

Please consult the section entitled, "Who May Apply?". If you meet these conditions, complete the Self-Assessment Guide to see if you have 55 or more points. If your self-assessment shows that you have a good chance to be considered, and you want to live and work in Manitoba, you should submit your application and necessary supporting documents to Manitoba Labour and Immigration.

What criteria are used to assess Provincial Nominee applications?

The criteria, as defined by Manitoba Labour and Immigration, include age, education, occupational demand in Manitoba, guaranteed employment in Manitoba, work experience, regional development, language and adaptability.

Do I need to engage the services of a representative (i.e. lawyer or consultant) to help me complete my forms or advise me on my application?

You are not required to have a representative. Some people do choose to have a representative;

however, if you hire someone, your application will not receive special attention, or be handled differently from other applications. Please see the brochure Immigration Representatives: Who they are and what you should know about them, included in this package or on our Web site: www.immigratemanitoba.com

Who do I include in my application?

Your spouse and all your dependent children must be included in your application. (See Important Terms for a definition of dependent children.) Your spouse and other dependent family members 18 years of age or over must complete the IMM 0008 and IMM 5406 forms.

What about my dependents who are not accompanying me to Canada?

All your dependents, whether they accompany you to Canada or not, must be included in Part A of your IMM 0008 application form. If they are 18 years of age or over, they must complete their own IMM 0008 and IMM 5406 application forms whether they are accompanying you to Canada or not.

Can my child, who is not considered a dependent according to CIC, come with my family to Manitoba?

Manitoba Labour and Immigration may issue Provincial Nominee Certificates of Nomination for accompanying adult dependents in order to facilitate the settling and retaining of the larger family unit in Manitoba. Certain conditions must be met for your adult dependent to be considered an accompanying family member under MB PNP. Consult "Who May Apply?" for details.

Can I claim my fiancé(e) as a dependent?

A fiancé(e) is not a dependent for purposes of immigration. If your fiancé(e) intends to accompany you to Manitoba, and you are not getting married before you apply for the MB PNP, he/she would need to fill out their own application and qualify on their own as a principal applicant.

Does it help if I have relatives in Manitoba?

Yes. If you or your spouse have a daughter, son, brother, sister, parent, grandparent, uncle, aunt, niece, nephew or first cousin in Manitoba, you will have a better chance of qualifying for the Manitoba Provincial Nominee program. Your relative must reside in Manitoba, be a permanent resident or Canadian citizen
who is 18 years of age or older, and may be required to sign an affidavit of support. Proof of that relationship will be required.

What if I have no relatives in Manitoba but other Manitoba residents have offered to assist me in settling in Manitoba?

Under the family-like support provisions, a group of five or more adults are eligible to commit support for a provincial nominee. The supporters must meet established criteria and sign an affidavit that they will support the applicant and any dependents for a minimum of one year. A copy of the affidavit is available
from Manitoba Labour and Immigration.

If my intended occupation requires licensing or registration, do I need to have all my work-related documentation in order before applying to the Manitoba Provincial Nominee program?

It depends on your occupation. Each province in Canada has different and strict accreditation requirements. Please research your individual case carefully. Consult our Web site, www.immigratemanitoba.com for links to sites that can give you more information.

Do my documents have to be translated by a certified translator?

All documents must be accurately translated into English or French for the Manitoba Provincial Nominee program. If nominated, the Canada visa office may require your documents to be translated by a certified translator.

I have a guaranteed job offer but my occupation is not on the Manitoba High Demand Occupations List for Provincial Nominees (HDOL-PN). Will I receive points for this job offer?

We recognize that there may be guaranteed job offers for occupations where you possess unique skills that are in demand, but the number of positions available do not warrant being listed on the HDOL-PN. There is a possibility we would consider giving points for your job offer, if your intended occupation is one
considered to be in demand in Manitoba. The employer may provide any available documentation to help determine that your employment will not take jobs away from Canadian citizens or permanent residents.

How do I qualify for points under Regional Development?

If there is a demonstrated connection to your destination, which is outside the perimeter of Winnipeg, you may qualify for points under Regional Development. You need to demonstrate this connection and prove to Manitoba Labour and Immigration that you truly intend to settle and work there. Proof may include, but
is not limited to:

- relatives in the area

- friends in the area

- other unique ties to the community

- experience living and/or working in a rural area

- a list of potential employers in the region who require your occupation in that region

- proof of direct contact between the applicant and the employer

- any other documentation to help establish this connection

How much money must I bring with me to settle in Manitoba?

Provincial nominees are expected to be financially self-sufficient when they arrive in Manitoba. The amount of available money that you need will depend on a number of factors. These include, but are not limited to whether you have a job in Manitoba, if you have relatives or other family-like support, or if your spouse has a good chance of finding work. We will ask for further information about your financial resources when necessary. It is your responsibility to convince Manitoba Labour and Immigration that you have sufficient support. As a general guide, the Government of Canada recommends that you have at least $10,000 (Canadian) plus $2,000 (Canadian) for each accompanying dependent.

Is there a deadline for applying to the Manitoba Provincial Nominee program?

No. However, the selection criteria may change without notice. The occupations that are in demand in the province of Manitoba may also change. Your application will be assessed according to the criteria in place at the time we receive your application.

What fees will I have to pay?

There is no fee for applying to the Manitoba Provincial Nominee program. If you are approved as a provincial nominee, you will have to pay all federal processing fees and Right of Landing fees that apply to each member of your family. Do NOT include fees with your Provincial Nominee application for skilled workers.
The federal fees, which are paid to the Canada visa office, should ONLY be paid if, and when, you are instructed to do so, by Manitoba Labour and Immigration.

Who assesses the applications for the Manitoba Provincial Nominee program?

Immigration program officers at Manitoba Labour and Immigration assess all applications. Each application is reviewed by at least two program officers.

If I am approved for the Manitoba Provincial Nominee program for skilled workers, what is my next step?

If you are approved as a Manitoba provincial nominee, you will receive a letter that explains the next steps. Successful applicants will be asked to submit their ORIGINAL application to a Canada visa office as soon as possible, and not longer than 180 days of being nominated by Manitoba Labour and Immigration.

NOTE: The first step in this two-step application process is to submit your Manitoba Provincial Nominee application to Manitoba Labour and Immigration (address indicated in this package). Those chosen for the Manitoba Provincial Nominee program will be instructed on how to apply for their permanent resident
visa through Citizenship and Immigration Canada, which has the final authority for issuing immigration visas. Do NOT send original documents to the Manitoba Provincial Nominee program.

PROVINCIAL NOMINEE APPLICANTS SHOULD NOT SUBMIT ANY APPLICATIONS OR DOCUMENTS TO A CANADA VISA OFFICE UNTIL THEY ARE INSTRUCTED TO DO SO BY MANITOBA LABOUR AND IMMIGRATION.

Will I require a medical examination or criminal and security clearance?

Although a medical examination, and criminal and security checks are not required to be approved as a Manitoba provincial nominee, they will be required before you can receive a permanent resident visa for Canada. A person who is approved as a Manitoba provincial nominee, his or her spouse and dependent
children, whether accompanying or not, will each need to have a medical examination. All adults will require a criminal and security check as well. Any related costs are the responsibility of the applicant. The medical examination and background checks are requirements of Citizenship and Immigration Canada.
Successful applicants will receive further instructions regarding how and when to complete these tasks. Manitoba will withdraw the PN Certificate of Nomination prior to the issuance of the Permanent Resident visa (IMM 1000) if:

- the provincial nominee, or any accompanying dependent, is found inadmissible as a result of medical, criminal or security checks, or

- Manitoba Labour and Immigration learns that information provided in the application is false or misleading.

DO NOT TAKE A MEDICAL EXAMINATION FOR IMMIGRATION PURPOSES UNTIL YOU ARE INSTRUCTED TO DO SO BY CITIZENSHIP AND IMMIGRATION CANADA. OTHERWISE, YOUR EXAM RESULTS MAY EXPIRE, AND YOU WILL HAVE TO PAY TO RE-DO THE EXAM.

How long will it take for me to receive a Canadian Permanent Resident Visa?

Applying for a permanent resident visa under the Provincial Nominee program is a two-step process. The first step is the assessment and decision made on your application by Manitoba Labour and Immigration. Information on current processing times is available by contacting Manitoba Labour and Immigration.

If approved as a Manitoba provincial nominee, the second step begins when you apply to a Canada visa office for a permanent resident visa. Citizenship and Immigration Canada attempts to process Manitoba provincial nominees as quickly as possible. While processing times can vary from post to post, processing times on average are significantly less for provincial nominees than for applications through the federal streams. A significant difference is that if all documents are complete, an interview by the Canada visa office may not be required for Manitoba provincial nominees.

NOTE: There is no guarantee that an interview will be waived; however, experience has shown this is more likely to occur if an applicant is supported by a Manitoba Provincial Nominee Certificate.

The following can delay processing of your application: incomplete or unsigned application forms; missing documents; insufficient postage; missing fees; unclear photocopies; documents not accompanied by a certified English or French translation; a medical condition that may require additional tests; involvement in criminal activity; family situations such as divorce, custody or maintenance issues; or failure to notify of a change of address. YOUR APPLICATION WILL BE PROCESSED FASTER IF ALL OF THE ABOVE ARE AVOIDED.

Who May Apply?

General: Skilled workers may apply if they:

• are 18 years of age or older when their application reaches Manitoba Labour and Immigration;

• believe, after completing the self-assessment guide, that they meet the selection criteria and can provide all the required supporting documents; and

• reside outside of Canada OR have proof of legal status in Canada*.

*Please be advised that Manitoba Labour and Immigration will only assess an application if the applicant and dependents (if applicable) are residing outside of Canada or can provide proof that they have legal status in Canada. For example, refugee claimants in Canada are not eligible for consideration.

Foreign temporary workers in skilled occupations may apply if they:

• have an employment authorization for work in Manitoba that was validated by Human Resources Development Canada. The current employer may be contacted to determine the need for permanent workers in that occupation, and/or a willingness to hire on a permanent basis.

Foreign temporary workers in semi-skilled occupations* may apply if they:

• have been working in Manitoba for at least 12 months in a semi-skilled job that was validated by Human Resources Development Canada;

• have an employment authorization for work in Manitoba that is valid for longer than 12 months, or one that has been renewed beyond the initial 12 months; and

• have a guaranteed job offer from their current Manitoba employer that meets the criteria as explained in the Self-Assessment Guide.

Semi-skilled occupations, for purposes of assessment under the MB PNP, have certain factors in common, including high turnover, frequent internal movement and on-the-job training. Semi-skilled occupations generally require two to four years of secondary school education (high school) along with short work demonstration or on-the-job training.

International students in Manitoba may apply if they:

- are 18 years or older when their application reaches Manitoba Labour and Immigration;

- have completed a course of post-secondary studies in a Manitoba educational institution;

- have completed at least six months of post-graduate employment (E08 Exemption) and are working in a study-related job; and

- have a guaranteed job offer in Manitoba that meets the criteria explained in the Self-Assessment Guide.

Accompanying adult dependents may be issued a MB PNP Certificate of Nomination if the principal applicant (parent) is approved as a provincial nominee and if the adult dependent:

- is between the ages of 18-25 and is not considered a dependent child by CIC;

- achieves a minimum of 25 points under CIC's skilled worker program;

- has never been married or had children of their own;

- is living with the principal applicant (parent) at the time the application is made; and

- will be travelling to Manitoba at the same time as the principal applicant.

Adult dependents who wish to accompany their families to Manitoba, and who meet the above conditions, should include an IMM 0008, IMM 5406 and supporting documents for those forms together with the parent's application.

MB PNP
http://www.gov.mb.ca

New Brunswick Nominee Program

Application Procedure

JOB OFFER APPLICANT

1. Complete the self-Assessment Score Sheet to determine if you qualify to be considered under this program. You must obtain a minimum of 50 points to proceed.

2. If you score at least 50 points, you should initiate a search for employment in New Brunswick. Finding and negotiating an offer of employment is your responsibility. Your application cannot proceed until you have a guaranteed job offer from a New Brunswick employer for work in New Brunswick.

Note: NBJobNet provides you with the opportunity to enter your resume in the provincial database of potential employees which is available to all New Brunswick employers. This is available online at http://nbjobnet.gnb.ca/

Your job search can also include using your links with professional or trade contacts, family, community or service groups.

More information on New Brunswick's labour market and useful tools for an employment search are found on our web site at: http://www.nb.workinfonet.ca/

3. For greater information about immigrating to Canada, obtain and read an Immigration Canada Guide for Independent Applicants: For candidates nominated by provinces under the Provincial Nominee Program and Kit for Independent Applicants which are available directly from the Canadian visa post serving your country or by internet, under "Applications" at http://www.cic.gc.ca.

4. When a job has been offered to you and you have indicated in writing your acceptance of the offer, the employer will complete a Guaranteed Job Offer Form (NBPNP 004). This form is included in the kit for your information or available from the New Brunswick Investment and Immigration.

5. You will now complete the application forms provided in this kit and gather required supplementary documentation for both the New Brunswick Supplementary Information Form (NBPNP 001) and for the Application for Permanent Residence in Canada (Immigration application Form -Independent -IMM 0008). Make the necessary copies for your spouse and dependents over 18 years of age. When the forms are completed, make photocopies of all forms and documents for your records.

DO NOT REQUEST A POLICE CERTIFICATE/CLEARANCE OR MEDICAL EXAMINATION AT THIS TIME AND DO NOT PREPARE THE PAYMENT FOR PROCESSING FEES OR RIGHT OF LANDING FEES. THESE WILL BE REQUIRED LATER. THERE ARE NO ADDITIONAL FEES FOR THE NEW BRUNSWICK PROGRAM.

6. Organize your forms and documents according to the Document Checklist. Place these in a sealed envelope and mail to the following address:

Investment and Immigration
Department of Business New Brunswick
P.O. Box 6000
Fredericton, New Brunswick

E3B 5H1

7. Your application will be assessed by New Brunswick Program Officers against the same factors and criteria listed in the self-Assessment Score Sheet. You will be advised in writing of the results of this assessment. If there is a difference between the score that you assign yourself and the score assigned by the New Brunswick Program Officer, the Officer's assessment will prevail.

8. Successful applicants will be contacted by New Brunswick Program Officers with further instructions, including requirements for Police Certificates/Clearances and Processing and Right of Landing Fees levied by Citizenship and Immigration Canada.

9. When all requirements have been met, the Department of Business New Brunswick will send a Nomination Certificate, along with your complete immigration application, to the Canadian Visa Office that serves your geographic area.

Please note that nomination under the New Brunswick Provincial Nominee Program does not constitute approval of your application for immigration to Canada. Final authority rests solely with Citizenship and Immigration Canada to issue immigrant visas.

BUSINESS PLAN APPLICANT

1. Complete the self-Assessment Score Sheet to determine if you qualify to be considered under this program. You must obtain a minimum of 50 points to proceed.

2. If you score at least 50 points, contact the Department of Business New Brunswick to discuss your business proposal and make arrangements for an exploratory visit to New Brunswick.

> Investment and Immigration
> Department of Business New Brunswick
> P.O. Box 6000
> Fredericton, New Brunswick
> E3B 5H1
> Tel: 1 -800 -665-1800 or (506) 444-4640
> Fax: (506) 444-4277

Your application cannot proceed until you have met with New Brunswick officials and have had your business plan approved by New Brunswick and deemed eligible for the Provincial Nominee Program.

3. Indication of approval of your business plan will be provided directly to the Investment, and Immigration Branch by New Brunswick officials.

4. For greater information about immigrating to Canada, obtain and read an Immigration Canada Guide for Independent Applicants: For candidates nominated by provinces under the Provincial Nominee Program and Kit for Independent Applicants which are available directly from the Canadian visa post serving your country or by internet, under "Applications" at: http://www.cic.gc.ca .

NB PNP

Document Checklist

IMMIGRANT APPLICATION FORM (IMM 0008)

Each family member over the age of 18 must complete his or her own IMM 0008 Form, whether they are accompanying you to Canada or not. Children under the age of 18 are included on the principal applicant's form.
Check that each person's form has been filled out completely, and signed.
Attach six (6) current photographs for EACH member of the family.
Attach additional pages, where necessary. Write IMM 0008 on the top of each additional page.

ADDITIONAL FAMILY INFORMATION (IMM 5406)

Each person who completes an IMM 0008 form must also fill out the IMM 5406. Check that it is complete and signed.
Attach additional pages, if necessary. Write IMM 5406 on the top of each page.

NEW BRUNSWICK PROVINCIAL NOMINEE APPLICATION FORM (NBPNP 001)

Only one NBPNP 001 form should be completed for the entire family. Check that the appropriate questions are answered in full and the form is signed by both principal applicant and spouse.
Attach additional pages, where necessary. Write NBPNP 001 on the to of each additional page.

NEW BRUNSWICK INFORMATION RELEASE FORM (NBPNP 002)

Complete and sign this form so that the Investment and Immigration Branch can work on your behalf.

EMPLOYMENT OFFER - JOB OFFER APPLICANT ONLY

Provide a copy of the letter or contract which offers you guaranteed employment with an employer in New Brunswick. The written offer should include position title, job description and job requirements. Include a copy of your letter of acceptance of the job.

IDENTITY/MARRIAGE INFORMATION

Include copies of all appropriate birth, marriage, divorce, proof of separation, and/or death certificates for yourself and your spouse. If there are discrepancies in these documents, please provide a sworn affidavit explaining the discrepancies. Also include a clear copy of your National Identity Card/Certificate or Cedula (where applicable).

CHILDREN'S INFORMATION

Include copies of each child's birth certificate (which names their parents); adoption papers; proof of custody for children under the age of 18 and proof that the children may be removed from the jurisdiction of the court. If the children will not be accompanying you to Canada, prove that you have fulfilled any obligation stated in a custody agreement. Submit proof of continuous full-time studies for all dependent children aged 19 or over. You must provide a letter(s) from the school(s), signed by a school official, confirming continued enrollment in full-time studies since turning 19 years of age.

PASSPORT/TRAVEL DOCUMENTS

Include copies of passport or travel documents that are valid for at least two years for yourself, your spouse and dependent children. Children must each have their own passport, separate from their parents. You are required to submit only copies of pages showing the passport number, date of issue and expiration, your photo, name, date and place of birth. If you reside in a different country than your nationality, include a copy of your visa for the country in which you currently reside. (Nationals of the People's Republic of China should note that Public Affairs Passports are NOT valid for immigration to Canada.) Include copies of entry or exit visas from previous visits to Canada.

EDUCATIONAL INFORMATION

Submit copies of educational degrees, diplomas or certificates for both the principal applicant and the spouse. Proof of education must include official transcripts showing school(s) attended, courses taken, degree(s) completed and photocopies of professional licenses. If the principal applicant studied in New Brunswick, he or she must provide proof.

EMPLOYMENT INFORMATION

Submit copies of letters of reference detailing both the principal applicant and the spouse's past and present work experience. Letters of reference must be on official letterhead and signed by an authorized representative of the company who is identified by name and title. Each letter should indicate:

> Specific period of your employment with the company;
> Position(s) you held, and time spend in each position;
> Your main responsibilities in each position; and
> Total annual salary during your employment

You may include any letter(s) or contract(s) about your employment or information you believe may be relevant to your successful establishment in New Brunswick. This may help to determine the suitability of your employment skills, as well as demonstrate your motivation, adaptability, initiative or resourcefulness.

PROOF OF RELATIONSHIP TO FAMILY IN NEW BRUNSWICK

Provide proof of your relationship to residents of New Brunswick, such as copies of birth and marriage certificates (showing the names of common parents). You must also submit photocopies of your relative(s) Canadian Passports, Certificates of Citizenship, or Immigration Visas (IMM 1000).
Omit this item if you do not have relatives in New Brunswick.

EVIDENCE OF VISIT TO NEW BRUNSWICK

Provide copies of previous visitor visas, accommodation etc. receipts, employment authorizations or student visas, if applicable

BUSINESS NET WORTH - Business Plan applicants only.

Complete the NBPNP 003, noting the need to have information validated.

SETTLEMENT FUNDS

You must prove that you have sufficient funds to maintain yourself and your dependents until you become established in New Brunswick. This includes bank account statements, letters from your financial institution, and other proof of liquid assets: i.e. funds that are readily transferable to a banking institution in New Brunswick. Your Personal Net Worth Statement (in NBPNP 001) must be supported by photocopies of evidence of ownership with an objective price value of real properties (land and buildings) that you own.

PUT All OF YOUR APPLICATION FORMS AND SUPPORTING DOCUMENTS TOGETHER AND FORWARD THEM IN A SEALED ENVELOPE TO:

> INVESTMENT AND IMMIGRATION
> DEPARTMENT OF BUSINESS NEW BRUNSWICK
> P.O. Box 6000

FREDERICTON, NEW BRUNSWICK
CANADA E3B 5H1

Additional documents may be requested to assist the evaluation of your application.

DO NOT SEND ANY FEES AND DO NOT REQUEST A POLICE CERTIFICATE OR MEDICAL EXAMINATION AT THIS TIME. WHEN YOUR APPLICATION TO THE PROVINCIAL NOMINEE PROGRAM HAS BEEN ASSESSED, YOU WILL BE CONTACTED WITH FURTHER INSTRUCTIONS.

NB PNP

HIGH DEMAND OCCUPATIONS

NEW BRUNSWICK PROVINCIAL NOMINEE PROGRAM

CNC Machine Programmers and Operators
Computer Business Analysis
Computer Systems Analysis
Design Engineers (Metalworking & Plastics Industry)
Design Technicians (Metalworking & Plastics Industry)
Electrical Mechanic
Electronic Service Technicians (household and business equipment)
Fabricators (Metalworking & Plastics Industry)
Financial Auditors and Accountants
Fitters (Metalworking & Plastics Industry)
Foundry Engineers
Graphic Designers and illustrating Artists
Hydraulic Technicians
Information Technology Instruction/Training
Information Technology Programmer Analysts
Information Technology Programmers
Information Technology Project Managers
Information Technology Marketing
Machinery Engineers and Designers
Machinist for Production of Molds used in the Plastics Industry
Medical Laboratory Technicians
Medical Radiation Technologists
Mold Makers for the Plastics Industry
Pharmacists Precision Machinists
Refrigeration and Air Conditioning Mechanics
Respiratory Therapists and Clinical Perfusionists
Software/ Application Development
Tool & Die Makers
Translators, Terminologists and Interpreters
Welding Engineers
Welding Technologists and Technicians

Frequently Asked Questions

Who is included in my application?

If you are married, either you or your spouse may apply as the principal applicant. Both of you should complete the self-assessment worksheet in this kit to determine which of you would get a higher point score and should therefore apply as the applicant. The other spouse will apply as a dependent. You must also include on your application form all dependent children whether they are accompanying you to Canada or not. You and your dependents must pass background checks and medical examinations. All family members 18 years of age or over must complete their own individual application form.

Should I pay someone to complete my forms and advise me on my application?

In some cases (for example, if you have difficulty understanding the form) you may wish to pay someone to help you fill in the information or give you advice. However, this does not mean that your application will receive special attention or necessarily be approved.

I cannot fit all the information on the application form and what if the information changes?

You should complete the form by printing or typing clearly and you must sign your application form. If you need more space to answer any questions, attach separate pages. When you have signed the form, it becomes a legal document and the information you have provided must be truthful, complete and correct. It is an offense under the Immigration Act to knowingly make a false or misleading statement. If any information changes before you arrive in Canada (even if your visa has already been issued), you must inform in writing the visa office to which you applied.

Do I need a passport or travel document?

You and your dependents must have passports or travel documents that are valid. If any documents are soon to expire, you should renew them. Diplomatic, official, service or public affairs passports cannot be used to immigrate to Canada. You must have a valid regular or private passport when you arrive. The validity of your visa may be affected by the validity of your passport.

Must I or others in my family attend an interview?

When your application for immigration to Canada is being processed at a visa office, a visa officer will review your application and decide if an interview is necessary. If so, you will be informed of the time and place. Your spouse and dependent children aged 18 or over will be asked to come with you. The visa officer may ask you about your job, work experience, education, reasons for migrating, plans and preparations. The officer may also ask about your family, spouse and/or dependents or your health, financial situation or past difficulties with the law. There may also be questions to determine your ability to settle successfully in Canada. Your answers will help in the assessment of your personal suitability, occupational expertise and professional qualifications, and to evaluate your motivation, initiative, adaptability, resourcefulness and overall ability to settle successfully in Canada. However, you will not be required to attend an interview for the New Brunswick Provincial Nominee Program application

Do professionals need registration and licensing to work in Canada?

In Canada, approximately 20 percent of occupations are regulated to protect the health and safety of Canadians (e.g. nurses, engineers, teachers, and electricians). People who want to work in regulated occupations need to obtain a license from a provincial regulatory body. Licensing requirements often include education from a recognized school, Canadian work experience and completion of a technical exam. Fees for exams can be costly and are the responsibility of the applicant. Final assessment by the provincial authority can only be done after you are in Canada with permanent resident status.

Will I have a medical examination?

A person who is approved as a Provincial Nominee, his or her spouse and dependent children will need to have medical examinations. All adults will require a background check as well. Any related costs are the responsibility of the applicant. The medical examination and background check are requirements of Citizenship and Immigration Canada. Applicants approved for nomination by New Brunswick will receive further instructions regarding how and when to complete these tasks.

DO NOT HAVE A MEDICAL EXAMINATION FOR IMMIGRATION PURPOSES UNTIL YOU ARE INSTRUCTED TO DO SO. OTHERWISE, YOUR EXAM MAY EXPIRE, AND YOU WILL BE ASKED TO HAVE IT DONE AGAIN.

Does it help to have a relative in New Brunswick?

Yes. If you or your spouse have a close relative in Canada, you can have a better chance of qualifying for the Provincial Nominee Program. Your relative in New Brunswick must be a permanent resident or Canadian citizen who is 19 years of age or over. You must provide documentation to prove the relationship.

What fees must I pay?

If you are approved as a Provincial Nominee, you will have to pay a processing fee for yourself and each member of your family when your application for immigration is submitted to the Canadian Visa Office. Instructions will be provided to help you determine the amount and how to submit it. The processing fee is non-refundable, even if your application is refused. The fees to be paid to Canada will also include the Right of Landing Fee (ROLF). The ROLF is required of every adult aged 19 or over in your family but, unlike the processing fee, is refundable if an immigrant visa is refused or not used, or if you withdraw your application. The ROLF can be paid at any time during the application process, but must be paid before an immigration visa can be issued. You will also have to pay other fees such as those related to the medical examination and police clearance.

DO NOT INCLUDE PAYMENT FOR ANY OF THESE FEES WHEN YOU SUBMIT YOUR APPLICATION FOR THE PROVINCIAL NOMINEE PROGRAM. YOU WILL RECEIVE FURTHER INSTRUCTIONS ABOUT SENDING FEES LATER. THERE ARE NO NEW BRUNSWICK PROCESSING FEES.

How much money must I bring with me to settle in New Brunswick?

The government of Canada recommends that you have at least $10,000 (Canadian) plus $2,000 (Canadian) per dependent. If you are a New Brunswick Provincial Nominee business plan applicant, you will have to have sufficient funds to implement the business plan and to sustain yourself and all your dependents.

How long will it take for me to receive a Canadian Permanent Resident Visa?

Processing times will vary. Certain things can delay processing of your application: incomplete or unsigned application forms, missing documents, insufficient postage, missing fees, unclear photocopies, documents not accompanied by a certified English or French translation, a medical condition which may require additional tests, involvement in criminal activity, family situations such as divorce, custody or maintenance issues, or failure to notify the visa office of a change of address.

YOUR APPLICATION WILL BE PROCESSED FASTER IF YOU AVOID THESE PROBLEMS.

For how long is my immigrant visa valid?

Normally, immigrant visas are valid for 6 -11 months. from the date of issuance. The validity date is based upon the earlier of your or your dependents' passport validity date(s) or of the medical validity date.

IMMIGRANT VISAS CANNOT BE EXTENDED ONCE ISSUED. IF APPLICANTS DO NOT USE THEM WITHIN THEIR VALIDITY THEY MUST REAPPLY FOR IMMIGRATION TO CANADA.

NB PNP

Newfoundland & Labrador Nominee Program

Documents Checklist

1. Immigrant Application Form (IMM 0008)

2. Additional Family Information (IMM 5406)

3. Self-Assessment Worksheet (PNP-NF- SA)

4. Information Release Form (PNP-NF-01)

5. Newfoundland and Labrador Supplementary Information (PNP-NF-02)

6. Identity/Marriage Information (Copies of Birth/Marriage/Divorce Certificates)

7. Children's Information (Copies of Birth Certificates)

8. Passport/Travel Documents

9. Education Information (Copies of Diplomas/Degrees/Certificates)

10. Employment Information (Copies of Verification Letters/ Resume/C.V/Work Related Training)

11. Business Experience or Management Background (Directorships/Company Ownership/Company Positions)

12. Financial Information (Copies of Personal Financial Resources/ Business Financial Statements)

13. Letter of Verification from Financial Institution - Personal Funds

14. Personal Net Worth Statement

15. Evidence of Visit to Newfoundland (if applicable)

16. Business Plan Concept (**Requirement for applications under the Entrpreneurial Skills Category)**

17. Employment Offer from Local Company **(Requirement for applications under the Occupation/ Skills Category)**

18. Copies of Correspondence from Embassies, i.e. Letters of Refusal from previous applications, etc.

NF PNP
http://www.gov.nf.ca

Frequently Asked Questions

What is the Newfoundland and Labrador Provincial Nominee Program?

The *Newfoundland and Labrador Provincial Nominee Program* was created through an agreement between the *Government of Canada* and the *Government of Newfoundland and Labrador*. It allows the Province to recruit immigrants in order to meet its industrial, economic and labour market needs. A person who is nominated by Newfoundland and Labrador can then apply for a permanent resident visa at a visa office abroad, under the immigration category of *Provincial Nominee*.

How do I apply for the Newfoundland and Labrador Provincial Nominee Program?

If your *Self-Assessment* shows that you have enough points, and you want to settle and work in Newfoundland and Labrador, you should submit your application to be assessed by an appointed *Program Officer*. Newfoundland and Labrador has a set of criteria for Provincial Nominees, each of which is awarded a certain number of points. *The criteria include age, education, intended occupation in Newfoundland and Labrador, guaranteed employment in Newfoundland and Labrador, work experience, language and adaptability.* You should complete the *Self-Assessment Guide* in this package to see if you have enough points to be considered for the *Newfoundland and Labrador Provincial Nominee Program*.

Provincial Nominee Applicants must not submit any applications or documents to a Canadian Visa Office until they are instructed to do so by the Department of Industry, Trade and Rural Development.

Will I need to have a medical examination?

A person who is approved as a Provincial Nominee, his or her spouse and dependent children, will ALL need to have a medical examination. The medical examination and background check are requirements of *Citizenship and Immigration Canada*. Any related costs are the responsibility of the applicant. Successful applicants will receive further instructions regarding how and when to complete these tasks. Do not have a medical examination for immigration purposes until you are instructed to do so by Citizenship and Immigration Canada.

Will I be subjected to background and other checks?

All adults will require a background check. Any *related costs are the responsibility of the applicant.* Background checks are based on the requirements of Citizenship and Immigration Canada and include security, criminality and medical checks.

Will I need to be registered or licensed to work in Newfoundland and Labrador?

Many occupations require registration or licensing to work in Newfoundland and Labrador, as a matter of course. If you have enough points in the selection criteria to qualify as a *Provincial Nominee*, you may apply, even if your occupation is regulated or requires licensing. A *Program Officer* will inform you of these requirements, if applicable.

How much money must I bring with me to settle in Newfoundland and Labrador?

The *Government of Canada* recommends that you have at least $10,000 (Canadian) plus $2,000 (Canadian) per dependent. The amount of money that you need to be selected as a Newfoundland and Labrador Provincial Nominee will depend on other factors, such as whether you have a job in Newfoundland and Labrador or if you have relatives who can support you. We may ask for further information about your financial resources, as necessary.

How long will it take for me to receive a Canadian Permanent Resident Visa?

Processing times will vary. Certain things can delay processing of your application: incomplete or unsigned application forms, missing documents, insufficient postage, missing fees, unclear photocopies, documents not accompanied by a certified English or French translation, a medical condition which may require additional tests, involvement in criminal activity, family situations such as divorce, custody or maintenance issues, or failure to notify the Canadian visa office of a change of address. YOUR APPLICATION WILL BE PROCESSED FASTER IF YOU AVOID THESE PROBLEMS.

If I am successful in obtaining 40 points on my self-assessment score sheet, am I guaranteed the support of the Government of Newfoundland and Labrador in obtaining Provincial Nominee Class status?

There are no guarantees. Obtaining the minimum score of 40, or any other score, *does not automatically qualify an applicant* to be a Provincial Nominee. There are a number of other factors to be considered by the Province before exercising its prerogative in nominating any candidate as a Provincial Nominee.

If I am currently applying for a Canadian visa under the Refugee Category, may I apply instead to the Provincial Nominee Class for consideration?

No. The *Provincial Nominee Class* has as its mandate the recruitment of individuals that have demonstrated skills over a period of years and possess other qualifications as required by the Government of Newfoundland and Labrador.

Are there any costs associated with making this application?

Yes. Once your application is complete it must be submitted to the address indicated on the cover sheet of this Application Kit.

Accompanying the application must be a bank money order or other certified banking instrument, payable to the Newfoundland Exchequer Account in the amount of $1,000 (Canadian). This is a non-refundable application fee and its payment does not in any way guarantee an approval of your application.

Am I required to visit Newfoundland and Labrador as part of this application process?

While the Applicant is not required to visit Newfoundland and Labrador as part of the application process, it is recommended that he or she do so in order to familiarize themselves with the local culture, the quality of life here as well as the many business opportunities which exist in the Province.

NF PNP
http://www.gov.nf.ca

96

Saskatchewan Nominee Program

Frequently Asked Questions

What is the Saskatchewan Immigrant Nominee Program (SINP)?

The SINP is an immigration program under which the Province of Saskatchewan selects individuals from other countries and nominates them to the federal government for landed immigrant status. SINP eligibility criteria are designed to meet the specific needs of the Saskatchewan labour market and economy.

How do I apply to the Saskatchewan Immigrant Nominee Program?

You must complete an SINP application in one of our three categories – Skilled Worker/Professional, Business, or Farm Owner/Operator – along with the appropriate federal application for your category. Your SINP and federal application will be reviewed by SINP program officers and, if you meet the SINP eligibility criteria, you will be nominated to the federal government. When you receive notice of your nomination, you must then submit the federal application to the appropriate visa office of Citizenship and Immigration Canada (CIC), who will review your file and will undertake health, security and criminality background checks.

Do I need to meet the eligibility requirements of federal immigration classes?

No. SINP's eligibility criteria will be used to assess your application. You will, however, be subject to the federal government's health, security and criminality reviews, and could be asked to supply additional information to CIC. In some cases, individuals may be approved under Saskatchewan's criteria that would be refused under federal immigration classes.

How long will it take to get a visa under the SINP?

Processing times vary, however, successful SINP applications typically receive visas considerably quicker than individuals applying through federal immigration classes. In the first two years of operating the SINP, the average time from making the SINP application to receiving a visa was about eight months.

Will I be interviewed by a federal immigration officer?

This is unlikely.

Where do I submit the SINP application?

The address can be found on the SINP application forms for each of the three categories.

Am I required to get a medical check done?

Yes. If you are nominated under the SINP, you will receive instructions from the Canadian visa office on how to get medical examinations done for you and your family members.

Will background checks be done on me?

Yes. SINP nominees and their adult family members undergo security and criminality screening by CIC, as do all other immigrants to Canada. This will occur when your nomination is forwarded to the federal government by Saskatchewan Immigration Branch.

What financial assets do I need under the SINP?

This varies between the three SINP categories:

- There are no financial requirements under the SINP Skilled Worker/Professional category but federal guidelines recommend that immigrants arrive with a minimum of $10,000 plus $2,000 for each dependent, or some other source of financial support in Canada.

- Business applicants should have financial resources appropriate for their business plans in Saskatchewan.

- Farmers are asked to prove a net worth of $500,000 (Can.).

I am eager to move as soon as possible. When should I make arrangements to move to Saskatchewan?

Applicants should not make arrangements to move from their current country of residence (e.g. quitting their job, selling their house or business) until they are notified by Citizenship and Immigration Canada that a visa is being issued to them.

I have applied for refugee status in Canada. Can I also apply to the SINP?

No. The SINP will not process any applications for individuals who are applying in any other immigration category, including a refugee claim.

I am working in Saskatchewan on a Temporary Work Authorization and may qualify in a SINP category. Could I be considered under the SINP?

Yes.

I wish to immigrate to Canada and am willing to invest in a business in Saskatchewan. Am I eligible under the SINP Business category?

Business applicants must show they intend to manage and operate a business in Saskatchewan, not just invest in it, and that they will live in Saskatchewan. Passive investments, that is, investment in a business without ongoing management responsibilities, are not eligible. Individuals wishing to immigrate as passive investors may apply under the federal Immigrant Investor Program administered by CIC.

Do I need to get my trade or profession credentials recognized in Saskatchewan before applying to the SINP as a Skilled Worker/Professional applicant?

You must provide documented proof of your education, training, occupational credentials and/or work experience that show you can become eligible to work in your occupation in Saskatchewan after your arrival. If necessary, SINP program officers may ask you to have your credentials reviewed by a qualification assessment organization or the regulatory body responsible for your occupation in Saskatchewan.

SINP
http://www.immigrationsask.gov.sk.ca

HIGH DEMAND OCCUPATIONS

SASKATCHEWAN IMMIGRANT NOMINEE PROGRAM

Agriculture and Agri-value:

Assistant Hog Barn Managers
Hog Barn Managers
Pork Production Technicians
Veterinarians

Value-added Processing and Manufacturing:

CNC Punch Machine Operators
Gear Design Engineers
Gear Grinders
Heavy Duty Equipment Mechanics (Journeyman Mechanics)
Machinists
Motor Vehicle Body Repairers
Specialty Welders/Fabricators

Synchrotron:

Beam Developers

Quebec-selected skilled workers

Quebec-selected skilled workers have the skills, education and work experience needed to make an immediate economic contribution to the province of Quebec and establish themselves successfully as permanent residents in Canada.

Under the *Canada-Quebec Accord on Immigration,* Quebec establishes its own immigration requirements and selects immigrants who will adapt well to living in Quebec. If you want to come to Canada as a Quebec-selected skilled worker, you must first apply to the Quebec government for a certificate of selection (Certificat de sélection du Québec).

Applying to come to Canada as a Quebec-selected skilled worker is straightforward. Consult this section to find all the information and forms you need to make your application.

The rules for applying as a Quebec-selected skilled worker are subject to change, so make sure you visit this site regularly if you are considering settling in Quebec as a skilled worker.

Before you apply, make sure you are familiar with the current application procedures. After you apply, make sure you return to this web page to find out about the steps that follow.

Why Quebec

Why choose Québec

Is Québec made for you? Are you made for Québec? Nothing is better than forming your own opinion by taking an exploratory trip here. If that is not possible, consult as many sources of information as possible. An immigration project must be well documented and planned. The more you know about Québec, the more you will be able to make informed decisions and the best choice for you!

Do you have a taste for Québec?

On average, Québec welcomes nearly 45,000 immigrants a year who come from about 100 countries and participate actively in its economic, social and cultural development.

If you are someone with a taste for Québec, here are various themes to explore:

Location and characteristics

Located in northeastern North America, Québec covers an area of 1,667,441 km^2. Its geographic size is equal to the combined size of Spain, Portugal, France, Belgium, Switzerland and Germany. Québec is bordered by the Arctic Ocean to the north, the United States and New Brunswick to the south, Newfoundland and Labrador and the Atlantic Ocean to the east and Ontario to the west.

A tapestry of lakes and rivers crossed by a great river

Fed by the St. Lawrence River, one of the world's longest rivers, Québec has 750,000 lakes and 130,000 rivers and streams that cover 10% of its area. Québec makes up 3% of the Earth's fresh water supply.

The St. Lawrence River flows eastward through Québec for more than 1,000 kilometres before entering the Atlantic Ocean. It is a reservoir of drinking water for Quebecers and one of the most important navigable waterways in the world.

This blue gold constitutes the primary source of energy and is a pillar of the Québec economy. More than 75% of the electricity consumed by Quebecers comes from hydroelectric generating stations located throughout Québec.

A garden of hardwoods and conifers

Forests are immense and found everywhere in Québec. Extending over seven degrees of latitude, they cover an area of 750,300 km^2 or nearly half the province. Sugar maples, yellow birch, beech, jack pine, balsam fir and black spruce grow successively from south to north in a variety of lush landscapes.

The forests play an important role in Québec from an economic, social and environmental standpoint. Ecosystems, rivers and wildlife are protected and the forests are managed and renewed in the interests of Quebecers of today and of the future.

A warm valley surrounded by open spaces

Given its immense territory, Québec is relatively sparsely populated, making room for great spaces with magnificent landscapes. The majority of its inhabitants live in the south of the province, along the St. Lawrence River valley. Since the very beginning of the New World, this majestic river has been a preferred gateway for developing the heart of the North American continent.

Population centres

Those who prefer city living can easily escape into nature. Although Québec is vast, it is not necessary to travel far to reach forests, lakes or mountains. Along with being close to nature, the cities have abundant green spaces for enjoying a wide range of outdoor activities. Quebecers have succeeded in building their cities in the country!

For people who choose rural living and seek the beauty and tranquility of a country environment, each region in Québec offers picturesque sites and a unique quality of life.

Large population centres
Montréal 3,635,733
Québec 717,641
Ottawa - Gatineau (Québec part) 280,323
Sherbrooke 163,713
Saguenay 152,950
Trois-Rivières 142,201

Climate

Québec has four very distinct seasons, moving from very hot summers to often heavy snowfalls in winter.

Quebecers have learned to adapt to life in a northern region. Whatever the season, the climate is conducive to a host of activities.

- In **spring**, young and old go to the sugar shack where maple sap is transformed into delicious taffy before their eyes.

- **Summer** brings many festivals in all regions. It is also the ideal season for water and outdoor activities and for enjoying hiking trails and the thousands of kilometres of bicycle paths in Québec.

- In **autumn**, nature is adorned in a symphony of colors. This is the season for picking apples and watching snow geese.

- **Winter** is a time for getting together during winter festivals and enjoying sports such as skating, skiing, snowmobiling and ice fishing. Each year, Québec City has an average of 107 days of snow, while Montreal has 76.

Environment

Québec owes its abundant natural resources and rich biodiversity to the immensity of its territory. In every season, the majestic scenery that can be admired in cities and rural areas expresses the pleasant way of life and instills Quebecers with pride and determination to preserve the quality of their natural heritage.

International agreements

Environmental problems affect the entire planet. Québec's dynamism in this area is illustrated in the fact that it has always been among the first to support major international agreements to protect the environment and resources that we all depend on. Some examples are the Montréal Protocol on Substances that Deplete the Ozone Layer, the Agenda 21 program, the Convention on Biological Diversity and the Framework Convention on Climate Change.

Social consensus

To preserve the quality of the environment, governments and businesses from various sectors of Québec socio-economic activity have implemented numerous prevention, clean-up, restoration, and recycling programs.

For over 20 years, Québec has had a formal procedure to evaluate and examine the impact of projects that could have major consequences on the environment. Provided under the Environmental Quality Act, this democratic process attempts to maximize public participation from Quebecers through public hearings or information sessions requested by individuals, interest groups, businesses or the government.

Québec expertise

On both the local and international scene, Québec is proud to showcase the initiatives and expertise that its corporations, business people and research institutions have developed to provide or foster the emergence of techniques, products and services that are both environmentally friendly and economically and socially beneficial. Moreover, several of Québec's environmental and engineering consulting companies have developed internationally recognized expertise and apply their know-how and resources in over 100 countries.

At the heart of the environmental question

Québec hosts numerous international seminars and conventions on environmental matters. The exchange of information and knowledge that occurs at these exceptional forums helps the advancement toward sustainable development. Montréal also stands out as one of the world's environmental capitals. Several prestigious government and non-government organizations have their head office or carry on intense activities here.

Immigration and pluralism

Québec is a pluralist society. The French majority of French descent coexists with an English minority of British descent, Amerindian nations and people of various origins and cultures who have come from other parts of the world.

From the arrival of the first European explorers until the more recent migratory waves, immigration has shaped Québec and contributed to building its future.

The Québec government relies on immigration to help Quebecers meet some of the challenges they have taken on, namely, demographic recovery, economic prosperity, perpetuating the French fact and opening up to the world.

To this end, Québec welcomes nearly 45,000 immigrants a year from about 100 countries who participate actively in its economic, social and cultural development. _Immigrant population by ten main countries of birth_

Québec welcomes immigrants from the four corners of the globe with their know-how, skills, language, culture and religion. The Québec government recognizes the enriching contribution of these immigrants. It encourages cultural exchanges and closer relations among all the communities. But to fully participate in Québec society, immigrants must adapt to their new environment. They must be prepared to understand and respect the fundamental values of the host society.

In Québec, a number of cultural community organizations have been established in different fields of activity to facilitate the integration of newcomers, encourage their participation in public life and strengthen the sense of belonging to Québec society. There are hundreds of organizations in the fields of business, social and community development, international relations, culture and recreation, media, scientific research, intercultural relations and religion.

Quebec-selected skilled workers: Who can apply

The Government of Canada and the Quebec government have an agreement that allows Quebec to select immigrants who best meet its immigration needs.

Under the *Canada-Quebec Accord on Immigration,* Quebec establishes its own immigration requirements and selects immigrants who will adapt well to living in Quebec.

If you want to come to Canada as a Quebec-selected skilled worker, you must first apply to the Quebec government for a certificate of selection (Certificat de sélection du Québec), the official document that shows that the Government of Quebec has accepted you for immigration to its province. Visit the website of the Quebec ministry that handles immigration for more information on how to obtain a certificate. You will find a link in the Related Links section at the bottom of this page.

After you have been selected by Quebec, you have to make a separate application to Citizenship and Immigration Canada (CIC) for permanent residence. A CIC officer will assess your application based on Canadian immigration regulations.

You will have to pass a medical examination and security and criminal checks. You can find more information on both of these topics in the Quick Find section on the right-hand side of this page. You must also show that you have enough money to support yourself and your family after you arrive in Canada. You can find more information on the funds you will need in the Related Links section at the bottom of this page.

Quebec-selected skilled workers are not assessed on the six selection factors of the Federal Skilled Workers Program.

Quebec-selected skilled workers: How to apply

Making an application to immigrate to Canada is straightforward. Follow the steps described below.

There are eight steps to apply to immigrate to Canada as a Quebec-selected skilled worker:

4. Obtain a Quebec Certificate of Selection.

5. Obtain and print the correct application kit.

6. Complete the application.

7. Determine where you must submit your application.

8. Obtain the instructions for the visa office where you will submit your application.

9. Calculate your fees.

10. Check your application.

11. Submit your application.

1. Obtain a Quebec certificate of selection.

If you want to come to Canada as a Quebec-selected skilled worker, you must first apply to the Quebec government for a Certificat de sélection du Québec, the official immigration document issued by the Government of Quebec. Visit the website of the Quebec ministry that handles immigration for more information on how to obtain a certificate. You will find a link in the Related Links section at the bottom of this page.

2. Obtain and print the correct application kit.

You can download and print the application kit from the Related Links section at the bottom of this page.

3. Complete your application.

- Fill out and sign the forms. Most forms can be completed on your computer. Print the forms after you complete them, because you cannot save them on your computer.

- If you do not want to complete the forms on your computer, you can complete them by hand. Print clearly, using black ink. You can also use a typewriter.

- Answer all questions carefully, completely and truthfully. Incomplete application packages will not be processed and will be returned to you.

- You must complete all the forms:

    - Application for Permanent Residence in Canada

    - Schedule 1: Background/Declaration

    - Schedule 5: Declaration of Intent to Reside in Quebec

    - Additional Family Information

    - Use of a Representative. It is not mandatory to fill out this form. You must complete this form only if you want to use a representative to help you apply.

107

Using a representative is a personal choice. More information on immigration representatives is available in the Quick Find section on the right-hand side of this page.

4. Determine where you must submit your application.

You must submit your application to the correct visa office. You must submit your application to the visa office that serves your country of nationality or the country where you have been legally admitted for at least one year.

You can find a list of countries and corresponding visa offices in the Quick Find on the right-hand section of this page. Select your country of residence or citizenship and you will be directed to the visa office responsible for your application. You must check the website of the visa office where you will submit your application, since application procedures may vary slightly from one visa office to another.

5. Obtain the instructions for the visa office where you will submit your application.

You can find the visa office instructions you need in the Related Links section at the bottom of this page. Print the forms and instructions required for that specific visa office. The instructions include information on medical examinations and the criminal and security checks you and your dependants will have to undergo. More information on both of these topics is available in the Quick Find section on the right-hand side of this page.

6. Calculate your fees.

You will have to pay the following fees:

- The processing fee for you and your dependants must be paid when you apply. It is not refundable, even if your application is not approved.

- Wait until your application is processed to pay the Right of Permanent Residence fee for you and your accompanying spouse or common-law partner, if applicable. It must be paid before Citizenship and Immigration Canada issues your permanent resident visa. This fee is refundable if you cancel your application, if your application is not approved or if you do not use your visa.

You will also have to pay fees to third parties for:

- your medical examination

- a police certificate, if you require one as part of your criminal and security check, and

- language testing, as required.

Information on how to pay your processing fee and your Right of Permanent Residence fee is included in the instructions for the visa office where you submit your application.

More information on fees is available in the Quick Find section on the right-hand side of this page.

7. Check your application.

Make sure your application is completed correctly, and that you include all the necessary supporting documentation. Use the checklist that is included in the guide (Appendix A) to make sure you have not forgotten anything.

The visa office cannot process your application if supporting documentation or processing fees are missing, or if your forms are not completed and signed. This will delay your application.

8. Submit your application.

Mail your application and your fees to the appropriate Canadian visa office.

Quebec-selected skilled workers: After applying

Your application will be processed at the visa office where you applied. The process may vary depending on the visa office. However, some processing steps are common to all offices.

- The application assessment process

- Processing time

- Medical examinations

- Criminal and security checks

- The decision on your application

- Change of address

- Confirmation of permanent residence

The application assessment process

After you submit your application, a Citizenship and Immigration Canada (CIC) officer will verify that you have submitted all the required documentation with your application. The officer will make sure you have:

- completed your application form correctly and signed it

- paid your processing fee

- included your certificate of selection (Certificat de sélection du Québec) and

- included all of the required supporting documentation.

If your application is not complete, the visa office will return it to you without processing it.

The visa office where you applied will send you a letter when it receives your application and verifies that it has been completed properly. The letter will tell you what you need to do and what happens next.

Processing time

The length of time it takes to process applications varies depending on where you applied. You can check application processing times in the Quick Find section on the right-hand side of this page.

You may be able to avoid unnecessary delays by:

- making sure all the necessary information is included with your application

- notifying the visa office of any changes to personal information on your application, such as your address, phone and fax numbers or a change in the makeup of your family

- avoiding repeated inquiries to the visa office

- ensuring that the photocopies and documents you provide are clear and legible

- providing certified English or French translations of original documents that you submit in other languages and

- applying from a country where you are a citizen or permanent resident.

Your application will be delayed if the visa office has to take extra steps to assess your case. Your application will take longer if:

- there are criminal or security problems related to your application

- your family situation is not clear because of a divorce or an adoption that is not yet complete or child custody issues that have not been resolved or

- the visa office that processes your application has to consult with other CIC offices in Canada or abroad.

You can check the status of your application online after the visa office has started to process your application. Select the *Check application status* button in the Quick Find section on the right-hand side of this page.

Medical examinations

You must pass a medical examination before coming to Canada. Your dependants must also pass a medical examination even if they are not coming to Canada with you.

Applications for permanent residence will not be accepted if an applicant's health:

- is a danger to public health or safety, or

- would cause excessive demand on health or social services in Canada.

Instructions on how to take the medical examination will normally be sent to you after you submit your application to the visa office. More information on medical examinations is available in the Quick Find section on the right-hand side of this page.

Criminal and security checks

If you have a criminal record, you may not be allowed to enter Canada. People who pose a risk to Canada's security are not allowed to come to Canada either.

If you want to immigrate to Canada, you and any family members over the age of 18 who come to Canada with you must provide police certificates to the visa office. You must submit the police certificates with your application.

You can find more information about criminal and security checks in the Quick Find section on the right-hand side of this page.

The decision on your application

After the province of Quebec selects you for immigration, a CIC officer will make a final decision on your application based on the current requirements for immigration to Canada. The decision will be based on several factors, including the results of your medical examination, and the criminal and security checks. The officer will also assess the proof of funds that you have provided, to ensure that you will be able to support yourself and your family when you arrive in Canada.

The visa office will contact you if it needs more documentation or if you are required to attend an interview.

If your application is approved, you will be asked to submit your passport to the Canadian visa office where you applied in order to receive your permanent resident visa.

Change of address

If you move or change your address, telephone number or any other contact information after you submit your application, you must notify the visa office where you submitted your application.

Confirmation of permanent residence

If your application is approved, the visa office will issue a permanent resident visa to you. Your permanent resident visa includes your Confirmation of Permanent Residence (COPR) and your entry visa. Your COPR will include identification information as well as your photograph. Please check the information on your COPR to make sure it is correct. It should be the same as the information on your passport. If there is a mistake on your COPR, contact your visa office.

You must have your COPR and your visa with you when you arrive in Canada.

Work Permits

Documents Checklist

Completed **"Application for a Work Permit"** (IMM 1295)

Your job offer letter or contract from your prospective employer, and the file number provided by Human Resources Development Canada (HRDC) to locate the Labour market opinion. Your employer should be able to provide you with this file identifier

Proof indicating you meet the requirements of the job being offered

If working in Quebec provide evidence of a valid **"Certificate d'acceptation du Québec"** (CAQ)

Proof of identity

Proof of funds available

Fee payment in an acceptable format. Verify acceptable methods of payment with the Visa office responsible for your area.
Note: Visa offices cannot accept fee payments from banks in Canada

"Statutory Declaration of Common-law Union" (IMM 5409) (if applicable)

Any additional documents required by the responsible visa office

CITIZENSHIP & IMMIGRATION CANADA

Frequently Asked Questions

What is work?

Work is an activity for which wages or commission is earned, or that competes directly with activities of Canadian citizens or permanent residents in the Canadian Labour Market.

What is a work permit?

A written authorization to work in Canada issued by an officer to a person who is not a Canadian citizen or a permanent resident of Canada. It is required whether or not the employer is in Canada. Usually, it is valid only for a specified job and length of time. A work permit may be issued based on labour market opinion (HRDC confirmation) or may be issued on the basis of other requirements.

What is an Human Resources Development Canada (HRDC) confirmation?

An HRDC confirmation is the opinion provided by Human Resources Development Canada (HRDC) to the officer which enables them to determine whether the employment of the foreign worker is likely to have a positive or negative impact on the labour market in Canada. An HRDC confirmation may be required in order for a work permit to be issued.

The HRDC confirmation process is started by the prospective employer who contacts HRDC to get a job offer form. When the form is completed and submitted, HRDC considers several factors, including the availability of Canadians and the offered wages as well as the economic benefit the foreign worker would bring. HRDC then provides advice to the officer.

The HRDC confirmation is typically given for a specific period of time, and the work permit will be issued to coincide with this period. Renewal of a work permit beyond the specified period will therefore likely require a new opinion from HRDC.

Who requires a work permit?

Anyone who is **not** a Canadian citizen or a permanent resident who wishes to work in Canada needs to be authorized to do so. Depending on the nature of the activity, in some cases the person is authorized to work by virtue of the Regulations themselves. But in most cases, he or she will need to obtain a work permit from Citizenship and Immigration Canada to work legally in Canada. You may obtain further details on persons exempt from obtaining a work permit by visiting our Web site or by contacting a visa office. The requirements to obtain a work permit are outlined in the following pages of this guide.

When should I apply?

You can apply for your work permit as soon as you receive written evidence of your job offer or contract of employment or as soon as you receive an HRDC confirmation. In cases where a HRDC confirmation is not required, you may apply when you have written evidence of your job offer from your employer.

What requirements must I meet to obtain a work permit?

You must show the officer that you meet the requirements of the *Immigration and Refugee Protection Act* and *Regulations.* You must also:

- satisfy an officer that you will leave Canada at the end of your employment;

- show that you have enough money to maintain yourself and your family members in Canada;

- be law abiding and have no record of criminal activity (you may be asked to provide a

Police Clearance Certificate);

- not be a risk to the security of Canada;

- be in good health (complete a medical examination, if required);

- produce any additional documents requested by the officer to establish your admissibility.

What documents do I need to apply for a work permit?

Complete the application form and provide the following documents listed below:

Important: Although the documents listed below are normally needed in support of your application, local requirements may also apply. **You must satisfy an officer that you will leave Canada.** Visit the local Web site of the visa office responsible for your area or contact their office to verify all required documents, before submitting your application.

Proof of identity

- a valid passport or travel document that guarantees re-entry to the country that issued it;

- two recent passport size photos for each family member (the name and date of birth of the person should be written on the back of each photo); and

Proof of employment in Canada

- Your job offer letter or contract from your prospective employer, and the file number provided by Human Resources Development Canada (HRDC) to locate the labour market opinion (confirmation). Your employer should be able to provide you with this file identifier,

- Evidence that you meet the requirements of the job, possibly including specific educational requirements or past work experience possibly outlined in a resume,

- Evidence of the Certificat d'acceptation du Québec (CAQ) issued by the Ministère des Relations avec les citoyens et de l'Immigration (MRCI), if you work in Québec or will be working in Québec. If you do not need a labour market opinion (confirmation) you will usually not need a CAQ.

In addition, note that:

- if you are not a citizen of the country in which you are applying, you must provide proof of your present immigration status in the country of application;

- if the government that issued your passport or travel document requires a re-entry permit this must be obtained before you apply for a Canadian visa; and

- additional documents may be required

Will I need a medical exam?

In some cases you will require a medical examination. If a medical examination is required, you will be informed by an officer who will send you instructions on how to proceed. A medical examination **may add over three months** to the processing of your application.

The officer's decision is based on the type of job you will have and where you lived in the past year.

If you wish to work in health services, child care, primary or secondary education, you will need a medical examination and a satisfactory medical assessment before a work permit can be issued

117

to you.

If you want to work in agricultural occupations, a medical examination will be required if you have resided in certain countries.

Are there any conditions on my work permit?

An officer may impose, vary or cancel conditions when issuing a work permit. These may include one or more of the following:

- the type of employment in which you may work;

- the employer for whom you may work;

- where you may work;

- how long you may continue to work.

May my spouse or common-law partner and dependent children accompany me to Canada?

Your spouse or common-law partner and children who wish to visit Canada must apply for permission to do so. As long as you all apply together it will not be necessary for each person to fill out separate application forms. List the names and other information about your family members in the appropriate space on the application. If you require more space, attach a separate piece of paper and indicate the number and letter that you are answering.

Family members are the immediate members of your family. Your husband, wife or common-law partner is your dependant. A common-law partner is a person of the opposite or same sex who is currently cohabiting and has cohabited in a conjugal relationship with you for a period of at least one year.

Dependent children may be your own children or those of your spouse or common-law partner. They must:

- be under the age of 22 and not a spouse or common-law partner; or,

- have depended substantially on the financial support of a parent and have been continuously enrolled and in attendance as full-time students in a post secondary institution accredited by the relevant government authority since before the age of 22 (or since becoming a spouse or a common-law partner, if they married or entered into a common-law relationship before the age of 22); or,

- have depended substantially on the financial support of a parents since before the age of 22 and unable to provide for themselves due to a medical condition.

Children included in the application must meet the definition of "dependent children" both at the time the application is made and, without taking into account whether they have attained 22 years of age, at the time the visa is issued to them.

Your spouse or common law partner and children must meet all the requirements for temporary residents to Canada. They must satisfy an officer that they are genuine temporary residents who will be in Canada for a temporary stay. They may be required to provide evidence that they are law abiding and have no criminal record. If your family member applies for a TRV, they must also meet all the conditions to obtain a visa.

Include them on your application by providing their names and other information in the appropriate space on the application form.

Important: You may be required to provide a marriage certificate and birth certificates for any accompanying family members. If you are in a common-law relationship and your common-law partner will accompany you to Canada, you may be required to complete the enclosed form, *Statutory Declaration of Common-Law Union* (IMM 5409). Also provide evidence outlined on the form to support your relationship.

If your family members wish to follow you to Canada at a later date, they must make a separate application for admission.

May my spouse or common-law partner and dependent children work in Canada?

In order to work while in Canada, your spouse or common-law partner and your dependants must apply for their own work permit and must meet the same standards, including the labour market opinion (confirmation), that regularly apply to a work permit issuance. They may, however apply for their work permit from **within** Canada. This guide does not provide general information about obtaining a work permit for your spouse or common-law partner or your dependants. For more details including definitions, responsibilities, and conditions of eligibility refer to the guide "Applying to change Conditions or Extend Your Stay in Canada (IMM 5217)". The guide may be obtained by visiting our Web site or once in Canada, you may contact a Call Centre listed under the Contact Information section of this guide.

May I leave, then re-enter Canada?

In order to return to Canada, you must be in possession of a valid passport or travel document. You also need to hold a valid work permit if you are returning to work in Canada.

If you are a citizen of a country that requires a temporary resident visa to travel to Canada, you will also need to be in possession of a valid entry visa to return, unless:

- you are returning to Canada following a visit only to the United States or St.-Pierre and Miquelon; and

- you return before the expiry of the period initially authorized for your entry or any extension to it, either as a visitor, student or worker.

Possession of these documents does not guarantee re-entry. All persons must establish that they meet all of the requirements of the *Immigration and Refugee Protection Act and Regulations* before being authorized to enter or re-enter Canada.

> **Note:** Citizens of the U.S. do not require passports or travel documents to enter or return to Canada. Permanent residents of the U.S. do not require passports or travel documents if they are entering or returning to Canada from the U.S. or St. Pierre and Miquelon. However, both must provide documentary proof of citizenship or permanent residence, such as a national identity card or an alien registration card.

Where do I Apply?

Please submit your application to the Canadian visa office responsible for your area for processing. You should consult the local Web site or office regarding accepted methods of submitting applications. (i.e. general mail, in person, by courier etc.)

> **Note:** If you are a citizen or permanent residents of the United States, Greenland, or St. Pierre and Miquelon you can apply for a work permit at a Port of Entry, but you must produce the confirmation of your offer of employment (i.e. detailed job offer) and have any other documentation required by the officer to make his or her decision when you arrive at the Port of Entry.

> Eligibility to apply at a Port of Entry does not overcome the need for the labour market opinion (HRDC confirmation) and the officer at the Port of Entry may be unable to issue your work permit if your prospective employer has not made the necessary contact with Human Resources Development Canada (HRDC).

What Happens Next?

Your application will be reviewed to ensure it has been completed correctly and contains all of the required documents for processing. After reviewing your application, an officer will decide if an interview is necessary. If so, you will be informed of the time and place.

If your application is refused, you will be informed in writing.

If your application is approved, you will receive a letter confirming the approval. This letter is not your work permit. When you arrive in Canada you must show this letter to a Canadian officer at the Port of Entry. The officer at the Port of Entry will determine whether you may enter Canada and how long you may stay. You must leave Canada on or before the date set by the officer or have your status extended by an officer in Canada.

> If you move or change your address, telephone or fax number before your application has been processed, you must advise us of this new information by contacting the visa office where you submitted your application

Temporary Resident Visa Exemptions

*Persons who do not require a visa to visit Canada include:

*Subject to change at any time

- citizens of Andorra, Antigua and Barbuda, Australia, Austria, Bahamas, Barbados, Belgium, Botswana, Brunei Darussalam, Costa Rica, Cyprus, Denmark, Finland, France, Republic of Germany, Greece, Iceland, Ireland, Israel (National Passport holders only), Italy, Japan, Liechtenstein, Luxembourg, Malaysia, Malta, Mexico, Monaco, Namibia, Netherlands, New Zealand, Norway, Papua New Guinea, Portugal, Republic of Korea, St. Kitts and Nevis, St. Lucia, St. Vincent, San Marino, Saudi Arabia, Singapore, Solomon Islands, Spain, Swaziland, Sweden, Slovenia, Switzerland, United States, and Western Samoa;

- persons lawfully admitted to the United States for permanent residence who are in possession of their alien registration card (Green card) or can provide other evidence of permanent residence;

- British citizens and British Overseas Citizens who are re-admissible to the United Kingdom;

- citizens of British dependent territories who derive their citizenship through birth, descent, registration or naturalization in one of the British dependent territories of Anguilla, Bermuda, British Virgin Islands, Cayman Islands, Falkland Islands, Gibraltar, Montserrat, Pitcairn, St. Helena or the Turks and Caicos Islands;

- persons holding a valid and subsisting Special Administrative Region passport issued by the Government of the Hong Kong Special Administrative Region of the People's Republic of China; and

- persons holding passports or travel documents issued by the Holy See.

CITIZENSHIP & IMMIGRATION CANADA

120

Live-in Caregivers

Main Features

1. EMPLOYEE (CAREGIVER)

Are you interested in working as a live-in caregiver?

The Live-in Caregiver Program allows professional caregivers to work in Canada. Caregivers are individuals who are qualified to work without supervision in a private household providing care for children, elderly persons or people who have disabilities. The live-in caregiver must live in the employer's home.

There are four main requirements you must meet to qualify under the Live-in Caregiver Program:

- You must have successfully completed the equivalent of a Canadian high school education. This requirement will help to ensure that if you apply for permanent residence after two years as a live-in caregiver, you will be able to succeed in the general labour market. Studies indicate that the majority of new jobs in Canada require at least a high school education.

- You must have six months of full-time training in a classroom setting or twelve months of full-time paid employment, including at least six months of continuous employment with one employer in a field or occupation related to the job you are seeking as a live-in caregiver. You may have gained your training or experience in areas such as early childhood education, geriatric care, pediatric nursing or first aid. You may also have completed your training as part of your formal education. This experience must have been obtained within the three years immediately prior to the day on which you submit an application for a work permit.

- You must be able to speak, read and understand either English or French at a level that allows you to function independently in a home setting. For example, you must be able to contact emergency services if required and to understand labels on medication. You will be unsupervised for most of the day and may be required to communicate with someone outside the home. A good knowledge of English or French will also enable you to read and understand your rights and obligations.

- You must have a written employment contract between you and your future employer. The contract defines your job duties, hours of work, salary and benefits. The contract also reinforces your employer's legal responsibilities to you. This requirement helps provide a fair working arrangement between the caregiver and the employer and provides both parties with a clear understanding of what is expected of them.

Live-in criteria

An important requirement of the program is that employees must live in the employer's home. The Live-in Caregiver Program exists only because there is a shortage of Canadians or permanent residents to fill the need for live-in care work. There is no shortage of Canadians or permanent residents available for caregiving positions where there is no live-in requirement.

The application procedure

Your prospective employer will submit a request to hire you to a Human Resources Centre Canada (HRCC). The HRCC will ensure that no Canadian, permanent resident or other temporary worker already in Canada is qualified and available to take the employer's offer of employment. Once the HRCC has confirmed the job offer, it will send the prospective employer a confirmation letter. This letter will instruct your prospective employer to send a copy of the confirmation letter to you. You and your prospective employer should check the visa office Web site for specific information about the next step: applying for a work permit. It is up to you and/or your employer to download the appropriate application forms from the Web site, complete them and send them with the application fee and supporting documents to the visa office.

You will be asked for your diplomas, school certificates or transcripts listing the courses you have taken. You could be disqualified from the program if you are not honest about your education, training and experience. You must provide information about your marital status and the number of children you have. This information will not affect the outcome of your application. You may be asked to attend an interview with a visa officer. If your application form is incomplete, or you have not submitted all the required documents, your application will be refused.

If the visa office approves your application, you will be given instructions for medical tests. When CIC officials receive proof that your medical results are satisfactory and that you have met all other requirements, you will be issued a work permit. A work permit is not a travel document. You must also get a passport and a Canadian temporary resident visa (TRV), if required. The requirement for a passport and temporary resident visa will depend on your country of citizenship

Because of an agreement between the Government of Canada and the Province of Quebec, there are differences in the way the program operates for caregivers who will be working in Quebec. For more information, visit the Web site of the ministère des Relations avec les citoyens et de l'Immigration (Quebec Immigration) at www.mrci.gouv.qc.ca.

The work permit

A work permit from a Canadian visa office will allow you to work in Canada as a live-in caregiver. The work permit is valid for one year, and you must renew it before it expires. You can get an application guide to renew your work permit by contacting a CIC Call Centre at one of the numbers listed at the end of this publication or by visiting the CIC Web site. You will need a letter from your employer stating that your job as a live-in caregiver is being offered for another year and a signed contract between you and your employer. Include this letter and a copy of the contract in your application to renew your work permit. You are authorized to work only for the employer named on your permit. However, this does not mean you cannot change employers for personal or other reasons. Both you and your employer should be aware that you are free to change employers while in Canada. Citizenship and Immigration Canada will not deport you for looking for another place to work. You must have received a new work permit before you begin working for a new employer.

Involvement in any illegal activity could result in the cancellation of your permission to work in Canada. For example, you cannot work for any employer except the one named on your work permit. You cannot accept employment for any type of work except as a live-in caregiver. You cannot work for a new employer, even for a trial period, until you have a new work permit naming the new employer.

The contract

A signed employment contract between you and your employer is a legal requirement of the Live-in Caregiver Program. Your employer must give you a copy of the contract. It is part of the documentation that you must send to the visa office when making your application to work as a live-in caregiver. You will also require a copy of the contract if you need to request a new work permit. Both you and your employer must clearly understand the conditions of your employment before signing the contract. The relationship between employer and live-in employee is like any professional relationship. It is important to clearly set out what each person expects of the other to avoid any misunderstandings about the conditions of the working relationship.

The objective of setting out the relationship in a contract is to get the fairest working arrangement possible for both you and your employer. A contract can help to avoid future problems by protecting your rights and providing a clear statement of your obligations. A contract is a written, detailed job description that also describes the conditions of employment, including the maximum number of hours of work per week, and the wage rate for those hours of work. Nothing in the contract should violate provincial or territorial labour laws, which establish minimum employment standards such as the minimum wage and overtime payment for additional hours worked.

To ensure that the contract is effective, think carefully about what it is for and how you will use it. Later in this booklet, we have provided an example of a contract to assist you. How closely you and your employer follow it in setting up your own contract is up to the both of you. Remember: your contract will indicate what job duties your employer expects of you and will help ensure that your employer fulfills his or her legal responsibilities to you.

You are protected

As a live-in caregiver, you have legal rights respecting fair working conditions and fair treatment under employment standards legislation in most provinces and territories. Nothing in your contract must violate these rights. Employment standards legislation may cover rights in areas such as:

- days off each week;

- vacation time with pay;

- paid public holidays;

- overtime pay;

- minimum wage;

- other protection, including equal pay, equal benefits and notice of employment termination;

- maximum charges for room and board.

Public holidays are days during the year when most workers, including live-in caregivers, can have the day off with pay or receive a premium if they work. In Canada, some common holidays are New Year's Day (January 1), Good Friday (Easter), Victoria Day (late May), Canada Day (July 1), Labour Day (early September), Thanksgiving (mid-October) and Christmas Day (December 25). Some provinces or territories have one or two additional public holidays.

Working conditions, such as minimum hourly wages, vary widely in Canada according to provincial or territorial law. It is your responsibility to find out what employment protection is offered by law in the province or territory where you are working. A list of ministries responsible for labour standards is included at the end of this booklet.

Other working conditions

You have the right to your privacy in your employer's home. For example, you should ask for a lock on the door of your room as well as a key to the employer's house. Off-duty time is yours to spend as you wish. Your employer cannot insist that you spend your own time in his or her house. You also have the right to refuse to do work that is not covered by your contract with your employer.

Your legal documents, such as your passport and work permit, are your private property. Do not give them to your employer.

If you need help

If your employer treats you unfairly, you can call or write to the nearest provincial or territorial labour standards office. These offices are listed at the end of this booklet. Your employer cannot penalize you for complaining to these agencies. The agency may ask if you have tried first to resolve the problem by talking to your employer. Your employer may not realize that there is a problem, and you may be able to solve it by letting your employer know how you feel.

In every province and territory, there are private and public agencies ready to offer encouragement, advice and help if you experience other difficulties such as stress, anxiety or any other problem. These agencies are usually listed in the telephone directory. In some locations, there are also professional support networks for live-in domestics or caregivers. A list of these support networks appears at the end of this booklet. There is usually no charge for these services. In some cities, there are telephone services that provide recorded information on legal matters free of charge.

Human Resources Centres Canada offer employment services. To find out which HRCC serves your area, consult the government section of your telephone directory or visit the Human Resources Development Canada Web site.

What is abuse?

Abuse can take many forms. It can include criminal acts such as assault, sexual assault or negligence; it can be human rights violations such as harassment, verbal taunting or behaviour towards you that is degrading or humiliating. It can be a threat or a false accusation by your employer meant to frighten you into not complaining.

The best protection against abuse is information. Be sure that you know your rights and what steps to take if something goes wrong. Depending on the nature of the incident, abuse may be an offence under the Criminal Code or a violation under provincial or federal human rights legislation.

Do not confront your abuser. Inform the police or the responsible provincial or territorial authorities and let them take care of the investigation. A domestic worker advocacy group may also be able to provide you with counselling and support in a situation of abuse. A list of these groups is provided at the end of the booklet.

Thinking about quitting?

You will improve your chances of getting another job if you have worked in one job for a considerable period of time. Before quitting your job (unless there are problems of abuse) you should try to solve your work problems by talking about them with your employer. It is reasonable for you and your employer to revise your contract periodically to be sure that it is suitable to both of you. Talk with your employer before taking any action to quit your job. If you decide to quit, give your employer enough notice so that arrangements can be made for your replacement. Check your contract to find out how much notice you have agreed to give your employer. However, you are encouraged to leave a physically abusive situation right away.

Breaking the contract

If you leave your job, your employer must provide you with a record of employment (ROE). Only your employer can get and complete this document. The ROE shows how many weeks you have worked and how much you have earned. You will need this record to apply for EI benefits. If you are not applying for EI benefits, keep your ROE in a safe place. It is your work record and can serve as proof that you have worked the necessary length of time to apply for permanent residence as set out in the Live-In Caregiver Program regulations. Your employer cannot refuse to give you a record of employment. If you are having difficulty getting your ROE, contact your local HRCC and ask officials to follow up with your employer.

Remember that if you change jobs, you must have another contract with your new employer.

Any live-in caregiver who decides to live out, or who accepts any other type of employment, can be disqualified from the program.

Applying for permanent residence in Canada

You must complete at least two years of employment as a live-in caregiver to apply for permanent residence in Canada. You must have completed these two years of employment within three years of your arrival in Canada. The two-year requirement does not include any extended time away from Canada. For example, if you go away on vacation for three months, that time will not be included as part of the two years of employment. In some countries, you may need to reapply for a temporary visitor visa before you return to Canada. If you leave Canada for more than one year or if your work permit has expired, you will have to reapply to the overseas visa office to return to Canada under the Live-in Caregiver Program. You are free to leave the program and return permanently to your home country at any time. However, you should give adequate notice to your employer.

If you apply to stay in Canada, you must complete an application for permanent resident status. You can obtain an application guide by contacting a CIC Call Centre or by visiting the CIC Web site. You must prove that you have worked as a full-time live-in caregiver for two years. As proof of your employment, you can use a statement of earnings or T4 slips and any other documentation that would help to prove your work record. If you have changed jobs since your arrival in Canada, you should have a record of employment from each of your former employers. You will not have an ROE for your present job. If you have used your ROEs to apply for Employment Insurance, HRCC staff can provide you with copies.

Your application for permanent residence in Canada will not be assessed on the basis of your financial situation, skills upgrading in Canada, volunteer work, marital status or the number of family members you have in your country of origin. However, you could be found ineligible for permanent residence if you, your spouse or common-law partner, or any of your family members have a criminal record or a serious medical problem.

Your application for permanent residence could be cancelled if you misrepresented your education, training or experience to the visa officer when you first applied under the program.

If you are a live-in caregiver working in Quebec, you will also be assessed by provincial authorities on additional criteria, including your knowledge of French. For further information, visit the Web site of the ministère des Relations avec les citoyens et de l'Immigration (Quebec Immigration) at www.mrci.gouv.qc.ca.

Family members

You can include your family members in your application for permanent residence. You and your family members can then obtain your permanent resident status at the same time. Your family members abroad will be processed for permanent residence at the visa office in their country of residence. They will not be issued their immigrant visas until you have received yours, provided that the entire family passes medical and criminal screening and all other requirements are met. All your family members must pass medical and background checks, whether they are accompanying you or not. You cannot be granted permanent resident status until all your family members have passed their medical and background checks.

You can obtain information about sponsorship and other immigration-related issues by contacting a CIC Call Centre or by visiting the CIC Web site.

2. EMPLOYER

Before you look abroad

If you want to hire a caregiver from abroad, we recommend that you contact your local Human Resources Centre Canada (HRCC). Be sure that you are familiar with the conditions of the Live-in Caregiver Program before spending time or money recruiting employees from abroad, and that the program is the best means of meeting your needs. Is it necessary that your employee live in? In Canada, there is no shortage of caregivers who do not live in. It may be possible to fill your position with a Canadian or a permanent resident if there is no live-in requirement. Your local

HRCC could help you locate such an employee. The HRCC may ask you to show that you have made reasonable efforts to hire a Canadian or a foreign worker already in Canada as a live-in caregiver. You must have sufficient income to pay a live-in caregiver and you must provide acceptable accommodation in your home. Your job offer must contain caregiving duties for a child, or an elderly or disabled person. A job offer for a housecleaner, for example, is not acceptable under the program.

If the Live-in Caregiver Program best meets your needs, remember that there are four main requirements your caregiver will have to satisfy to qualify under the program. These requirements are listed in the Employee (Caregiver) section of this booklet.

How to hire a foreign live-in caregiver

Employers are responsible for finding foreign live-in caregivers through advertisements, personal contacts or hiring agencies. When you have found an individual you wish to employ, contact your local HRCC, which will assess your offer of employment. You will be asked to declare that you can provide the wages, benefits and working conditions required by provincial or territorial labour laws. The HRCC will provide information on acceptable wage standards, taxation, health insurance, workers' compensation and other relevant matters. Remember that the minimum wage in your province or territory may be below the market wage in your community. You should be prepared to pay a wage rate and provide benefits comparable to those provided to other caregivers in your community if you want to keep your employee.

When the HRCC has confirmed your offer of employment, you will be given a letter of confirmation. The letter contains important information about immigration for live-in caregivers, including the work permit application process. It will also advise you of the documents which you must send to your prospective employee as part of the caregiver's application process.

If your potential employee is considered eligible for the Live-in Caregiver Program and meets all other requirements, the caregiver will be issued a work permit. This process may take several months, so plan ahead. Even if the HRCC approves your offer of employment, your caregiver cannot work in Canada until he or she receives the work permit naming you as the employer. We suggest that you maintain contact with your prospective employee to determine when he or she will be able to begin working for you.

If you live in the province of Quebec, and if Quebec will be your employee's province of employment, your HRCC will be able to inform you of any differences that apply to the process of hiring a foreign live-in caregiver. For further information, visit the Web site of the ministère des Relations avec les citoyens et de l'Immigration (Quebec Immigration) at www.mrci.gouv.qc.ca.

Live-in caregivers have the right to change jobs without their employer's permission as long as they remain live-in caregivers. They are also eligible to apply for an open work permit after working for two years as live-in caregivers in Canada.

Employer's responsibility to a live-in employee

You must provide acceptable working conditions, reasonable duties and fair market wages. You must also provide accommodation that ensures privacy, such as a private room with a lock on the door. Your caregiver pays rent for a room in your home and is entitled to privacy. You should not enter the caregiver's room without permission. You should provide your employee with a key to the house to ensure freedom of access. Your house is your employee's home as well as his or her place of work. You should respect the caregiver's cultural or religious practices and discuss his or her needs.

A live-in caregiver is protected by employment standards legislation in most provinces and territories. Live-in employees are entitled to days off each week, statutory holidays, extra pay for overtime work and a salary that meets at least the minimum wage. It is your responsibility to find out what these standards are and to respect the laws of your province or territory. A list of ministries responsible for labour standards is provided at the end of this booklet.

Hiring a caregiver who is already in Canada

You may wish to hire a live-in caregiver who is already in Canada as a temporary worker under the program but is unemployed. Your offer of employment must first be confirmed by an HRCC. Give a copy of the letter from the HRCC which confirms your job offer to the caregiver you wish to hire. The caregiver needs this letter to apply for a new work permit naming you as the employer. The caregiver must have received the new work permit before starting work in your home. It is illegal for the caregiver to work without a valid work permit naming you as the employer. Trial employment is not allowed. It is illegal to employ a caregiver on a trial basis to determine if the caregiver is suitable for a one-year contract. You could be charged with a criminal offence for employing a worker who is not authorized to work by Citizenship and Immigration Canada (CIC).

Employer's legal responsibilities

Anyone who employs a full-time live-in caregiver under the program is required by federal law to register as an employer with the Canada Customs and Revenue Agency (CCRA). You must make the proper deductions for income tax, Employment Insurance and Canada Pension Plan and remit these amounts to the proper federal authority. When you register as an employer, the CCRA will provide you with an information guide which contains the necessary forms and instructions. You must comply with the law and provide your employee with a record of employment (ROE) when the employee's work term with you has ended. You will not be able to get the ROE unless you have previously registered as an employer.

Like all other small business employers in Canada, you must keep written records of your caregiver's employment. Employment standards laws require that records of an employee's earnings be kept and that employees be provided with a statement of earnings with each pay cheque. The statement should indicate your employee's gross and net pay, specific deductions, the purpose of these deductions, and the total hours worked (including overtime) during that pay period.

You are also required by law to give your employee a T4 slip for the previous year's employment by the end of February each year. The T4 slip will show your employee's total gross earnings and total deductions for income tax purposes. Your employee will require the T4 to file an annual income tax return. The CCRA will give you an information guide on tax requirements when you register as an employer.

Room and board

Charges for meals not eaten by your employee in your home cannot be deducted from his or her pay. Room charges are calculated on a weekly or monthly basis, depending on the conditions of the employment contract. Whether you may deduct room and board directly from your employee's pay cheque may also be governed by provincial or territorial employment standards legislation.

Your employee is entitled to leave your home on days off.

Ending a contract with an employee

If your employee is unwilling or unable, without just cause, to perform the job duties as stated in the contract, and you no longer wish to employ the caregiver, you can terminate the contract. However, you may have agreed in the contract to give a notice of termination. When you cannot give the caregiver appropriate notice, you can pay the employee for the period the notice would have covered. Regardless of whether your contract requires you to give notice or pay in lieu of notice, you may be liable for it under provincial or territorial laws.

You are required to notify the nearest HRCC if you no longer need the services of your caregiver.

If you abuse the terms of the contract, you will have difficulty hiring another live-in caregiver under the program. If you need to find a replacement for your employee, you must repeat the Live-in Caregiver Program's application procedure.

Documents Checklist

- *In-Canada Application for Permanent Residence* (IMM 5002)

- Two (2) photocopies (three (3) if you live in Quebec) of the *In Canada Application for Permanent Residence* (IMM 5002) form

- *Authority to Release Information to Designated Individuals* (IMM 5476), if applicable

Photocopies of the following items: (Photocopies do not need to be certified.)

- Passport pages for you and any dependants in Canada clearly showing the passport number, name, date of birth, passport issue/expiry date, entry and exit stamps, visas for Canada and any other countries, and stamp made by a Canadian authority showing most recent entry into Canada

- Birth certificates or baptismal certificates for you and all your dependants

- Marriage certificate, if applicable

- Proof of your common-law relationship (e.g., evidence of joint bank, trust, credit union or charge card accounts; jointly signed residential lease, mortgage or purchase agreement; statutory declarations of individuals with personal knowledge that your relationship is genuine and continuing), if applicable

- Divorce, annulment or death certificates, if you were previously married

- Custody papers for dependent children from a previous marriage/relationship

- Proof of medical examination results, if applicable

Original documents:

- Police Certificate(s)

- Certified translations for **all** documents (e.g. police, birth certificates, etc.) that are not in English or French

- Proof of two years of authorized full-time employment as a live-in caregiver

    - Signed and dated letter from current employer indicating the day, month and year you began working for him or her

    - Signed and dated letter from all previous employers indicating start and finish dates (day, month and year)

    - Record of Employment for all previous employers

    - Notice of Assessment which can be obtained by calling Revenue Canada

Photographs:

- Two (2) passport-sized photos of you and any dependants in Canada stapled to the "In-Canada Application for Permanent Residence" (IMM 5002) form. Make sure names are written on the back. (Passport-sized photos for your spouse or common-law partner and dependent children over 18 who are in Canada should be attached to their application form.)

Processing Fees

• Copy 2 of the *Receipt* form that has been stamped by a bank or credit union showing the amount paid. (No other form of payment is acceptable.) (Include fee for work permit if you are applying for one.)

This *Document Checklist* (IMM 5282)

You have addressed the envelope with correct postage to:
Case Processing Centre, Vegreville, AB, T9C 1W3

CITIZENSHIP & IMMIGRATION CANADA

Frequently Asked Questions

A **permanent resident** is a person who can live in Canada permanently but who is not a Canadian citizen. A **live-in caregiver** is a person who:

- was approved to participate in the Live-in Caregiver Program at a visa office outside of Canada; and,

- has a valid work permit to work as a live-in caregiver for children, the elderly or the disabled with an employer in Canada.

Who may apply?

You may apply for permanent residence as a live-in caregiver if you:

- are living in Canada;

- have a valid work permit to work as a live-in caregiver;

- have completed two years of authorized full-time employment as a live-in caregiver within three years from the date you entered Canada under the Live-in Caregiver Program;

- have lived in your employer's home;

- told the truth about your education or training when you first applied for a work permit as a live-in caregiver; and,

- are able to support yourself and your family members without the need for social assistance or welfare.

Also, you and any family members must:

- pass an immigration medical examination;

- pass criminal and security clearances;

- not be the subject of an immigration inquiry or appeal; and,

- have valid passports or travel documents.

Note: If you live in Quebec, your application must also be approved by the provincial immigration authority, called the *Ministere des relations avec les citoyens et de l'immigration* (MRCI). You do not need to fill out any forms; we will apply on your behalf. If the MRCI approves your application, it will give you a *Certificat de sélection du Québec,* which grants you permanent resident status in Quebec. If the MRCI refuses your application, you will be given the opportunity to apply in another province.

Proof of two years as a live-in caregiver

In order to prove that you have worked in Canada as a live-in caregiver for two years in the three years since you first came as a live-in caregiver, you must attach all the items listed in the **Original Documents** section of the *Document Checklist* (IMM 5282).

Do not submit your application until you have fully completed the required 24 months of authorized employment as a live-in caregiver. If you do, your application will be returned to you.

Mailing your application

Send your application to us once you have read and followed **all** the instructions in the guide and attached all the items on the *Document Checklist* (IMM 5282).

Send everything in a 23 cm x 30.5 cm (9" x 12") envelope. Address the envelope to:

Case Processing Centre
Vegreville, AB
T9C 1W3

Be sure to include a return address. The envelope will require more postage than a normal letter. To avoid having your application returned to you, have the post office weigh it before mailing. Do not include prepaid return envelopes.

What happens after I have mailed my application?

If you have completed your application properly, it will be reviewed by an immigration officer and a letter will be sent to you within 90 days. The letter will let you know if your application was approved for processing in Canada, refused, or referred to a Canada Immigration Centre for further review. If you have not heard anything after 90 days, phone a Call Centre as indicated on the Contact Information page.

If you have not completed your application properly or have left out information, your application will be returned to you.

If you and your family members meet all immigration requirements, we will contact you to arrange an interview. You and your family members in Canada will likely be given your permanent residence at that time. Once you are a permanent resident, if you indicated that family members outside of Canada will join you immediately, we will let the visa office know to issue permanent resident visas to them. If you indicated that your family members will not be joining you at this time, we will take no further action.

How do I find out what is happening with my application?

Once you have received acknowledgement from our office that your application has been received, you can find out the status of your application by logging on to our Web site at www.cic.gc.ca. Click on the heading, "on-line services" and go to "E-Client Application Status". From there, follow the instructions to check your status. If you do not want the status of your application on the Internet, you can remove it by selecting the appropriate check box.

You may also check your status or remove access from the Internet by phoning a Call Centre.

What if I move or need to update information on my application?

If you have mailed your application and you move or need to provide new information, you should phone the nearest Call Centre immediately. New information may be that: answers to questions on the application for permanent residence change, you are convicted of a criminal offence, or you no longer want to continue with your application.

Becoming a permanent resident

Generally, it takes 10 months for single applicants and 18 months for applicants with overseas family members to have their applications processed. (These processing times are only applicable for applications that were completed correctly, signed and had all the required documents attached and fees paid.) We have no control over the time it takes to complete medical, criminal and security checks. These checks may cause processing times to increase.

To ensure that you have legal status in Canada, you should apply to extend your immigration status while your application for permanent residence is in process. You have legal status for the period of time indicated on a visitor document (work permit, study permit, visitor record) or temporary resident permit. Use the guide, *Applying to Change Conditions or Extend Your Stay in Canada* to apply for an extension. You should apply for your extension at least two months before your immigration status expires.

Working for other employers

Your current work permit allows you to work as a live-in caregiver for a specific employer. You may continue to work for this employer for the duration of the work permit. However, if you want to work for someone else or in another occupation, you must apply for a new work permit. You will need the guide *Applying to Change Conditions or Extend Your Stay in Canada*.

It is illegal to work without a valid permit.

Studying

If you wish to take a course that is longer than six months, you will need a study permit. To apply for a study permit, you will need the guide, *Applying to Change Conditions or Extend Your Stay in Canada*. If you take a course that is six months or less, you do not need a study permit.

If you already have a study permit, you may continue to study for the duration of the document.

Leaving Canada

If you leave Canada while your application is being processed, we cannot guarantee that you will be allowed to re-enter. This is especially true if you need a Canadian temporary resident visa (a visa affixed to a page in your passport).

What if my application is refused?

If your application is refused, you will be sent a letter. You will be advised to leave Canada before your current work permit expires. The processing fee will not be refunded. If you paid the right of permanent residence fee, it will be refunded.

Your application may be refused if you or your family members do not meet immigration requirements.

Some examples are: you do not qualify as a live-in caregiver, you or your family members do not pass criminal or security checks, you do not have enough money to support yourself and your family members, or you or your family members do not pass medical examinations.

CITIZENSHIP & IMMIGRATION CANADA

Medical Examination Instructions

1. REQUIREMENTS

Immigration Canada requires you to have a medical examination. To do this, you need to arrange for an appointment with a designated medical practitioner (DMS)

Note: You must have your medical examination performed by one of the doctors. If you do not follow the instructions, you may have to take another medical examination and pay the fees again.

The doctor will require all applicants who are over 10 years old to have a chest X-ray. An x-ray is required by children under 10 if there is a history or clinical examination which indicates there is need or if there is evidence of tuberculosis in the family. You will receive instructions from the doctor.

You must take with you to the doctor's office: your passport, your client ID# if known, your eye glasses, any relevant medical report(s), and four recent passport size photographs showing head and shoulder for each member of the family required to undergo a medical examination.

All costs related to the Medical Examination are your responsibility

It is possible that you may be asked to take further tests before a final medical decision is made. The costs of these further tests are your responsibility and over and above the cost of the medical examination.

2. PROCEDURES FOR ALL PERSONS REQUIRING A MEDICAL EXAM.

Make an appointment with a doctor from the list of designated medical practitioners. Check the list for a doctor nearest to where you live.

The medical examination, blood test, urinalysis and chest x-ray should be forwarded by the examining doctor, preferably by Registered Mail to:

Citizenship and Immigration
Immigration Health Services (RNH)
Jean Edmond Towers South
365 Laurier Avenue West, 14th Floor
Ottawa, Ontario
K1A 1L1

The medical parcel should be identified with the applicant's postal address. When the medical result have been reviewed Immigration Health Services will enter them into the computerized system. You should allow at least 6 weeks from the time of mailing for the results to be entered into the system.

If there is no Designated Medical Practitioner within 200km. (150 miles) of where you reside, you should contact the nearest Immigration /Visa office for permission to use a local doctor. The Canada Immigration Centre (CIC) can mark on the IMM. 1017 "Permission given to use a local doctor".

CANADA'S MEDICAL ADMISSIBILITY CRITERIA

All immigrants and certain categories of visitors who are seeking admission to Canada must satisfy Canada's medical admissibility criteria. In order to determine your medical admissibility to Canada, you and all of your dependent family members (if applicable) are required to undergo a medical examination. Enclosed for this purpose you will find Citizenship and Immigration Canada "Medical Report" form(s). Please check the accuracy of all information printed on the attached

134

medical form. If there are any errors, please advise us by fax or letter showing your file number.

The Medical Report form was recently revised. The latest version of the Medical Report consists of five sections, A to E. You have only received Section A, "Client Identification and Summary. " Sections B to E of the Medical Report form are for use by a medical doctor and are provided to physicians by the Department of Citizenship and Immigration, Health Services.

The medical examination must be performed by one of the licensed physicians shown on the enclosed "List of designated Medical Practitioners" (i.e. doctors). All family members should be examined by the same doctor. I f you, or any of your dependents are outside of your home country for an extended period of time, you may see another Designated Medical Practitioner (DMP). If you do not find the applicable country, please contact our office by fax or mail to request the appropriate list.

Your medical examination reports and X-rays must be sent by the Designated Medical Practitioner to the following address:

Director, Health Programs (RNH)
Citizenship and Immigration Canada
Jean Edmond Towers South,
14th Floor, 365 Laurier Avenue West
Ottawa, Ontario
K1A 1L1
Canada

INFORMATION FOR PHYSICIANS AND RADIOGRAPHERS PERFORMING MEDICAL EXAMINATION FOR CANADIAN IMMIGRATION (to be attached by Visa Office to all Medical Report forms IMM1017)

New Information (December, 1998):

The Medical Report form, IMM 1017 (see bottom of form), is the first page of a seven-page document. The first page is titled "Section A, Client Identification & Summary.' There are six additional pages which contain Sections B through E of the Medial Report form. The six additional pages, also known as form IMM 5419, are sent in CD ROM format directly to Designated Medical Practitioners by the Director of Immigration Health Programmes (address below) for Citizenship and Immigration Canada.

Generally, applicants for immigration are only given Section A of the Medical Report form and do not receive Sections B to E. You should have copies of the form IMM 5419, which contains Sections B to E. If you do not, please write to the Director of Immigration Health Programmes, at the address below, for information on how to obtain the form IMM 5419 on CD ROM.

Procedures for medical examination:

1. The person presenting this form requires the following medical tests:

· Complete medical examination - for persons of all ages

· Chest x-ray and report - for persons 11 years of age and over

· Urinalysis - for persons 5 years of age and over

· Syphilis serology - for persons 1 5 years of age and over

2. The results of the examination must be reported on form IMM 1017 AND form IMM 5419. Form IMM 1017 + Form IMM 5419 = one Medical Report. One complete Medial Report is required for each person examined

3. Actual laboratory reports are required

Procedures for x-ray

1. The radiographer will assure himself as to the identity of the person to be x- rayed and will inscribe, over his or her signature, the name of the person, the date of the x-ray and passport number, if available, at the center bottom of the film. Care MUST be taken to ensure that the picture of the lung tissue is not obscured.

2. In his or her report, the doctor reading the chest x-ray will describe all abnormalities in the x-ray film. The report is to be signed by the doctor who will also indicate his or her office address and identify the report as relating to the film and the person concerned.

3. Large x-ray films are required, corresponding to the standard sizes of diagnostic films (35 x 43 cm).

4. The following are NOT acceptable:

· a photograph of an x-ray

· a report based on fluoroscopic examination only

· an x-ray film that is technically unsatisfactory

· a film which does not demonstrate the entire chest

· a film more than one month old at time it is received by Immigration Health Programs in Ottawa

· a report without the film upon which the report is based

· a positive film or print

Packing and mailing the medical information:

1. The x-ray film and report, laboratory and medical reports are to be suitably packaged (not rolled) to avoid damage in transit. It is mandatory that the examining physician send all documents and chest x-ray(s) directly to the following address:

Director, Health Programmes (RNH)
Citizenship and Immigration Canada
Jean Edmond Towers South, 14th floor
365 Laurier Avenue West
Ottawa, Ontario, K1A 1L1
Canada

Note: Under no circumstances should any document or chest x-ray be given to the applicant!

2. The contents of the parcel are to be identified with the applicant's complete postal address, the address of the Immigration/Visa Office dealing with the application (found at the bottom of this page), and the file number (see box labelled "Visa Office & Number" in the upper right corner of form IMM 1017). The chest x-ray film and reports become the property of the Department of Citizenship and Immigration Canada and are NOT returnable.

ALL APPLICANTS SHOULD NOTE THE FOLLOWING

1. All fees related to this medical examination are your responsibility.

2. Please bring the following to your medical appointment:

- one recent colour passport size photograph of each family member if not already provided

- eye glasses (if applicable), list of prescription drugs taken or any relevant medical report(s)

- original passport(s) or other proof of identity

3. An applicant who has passed his or her 11th birthday must obtain a standard X-ray film of the chest with a radiologist's report. An X-ray film of the chest and radiologist's report is required for children under the age of 11 years if the medical history or clinical examination of the child indicates there is a need, or if there is evidence of tuberculosis in the family.

4. The issuance of these instructions does not constitute acceptance of your application. You should not make any commitments related to the application until your case has been concluded. **DO NOT DISPOSE OF PROPERTY OR EFFECTS, OR GIVE UP EMPLOYMENT OR ACCOMMODATION OR TAKE OTHER SIMILAR STEPS TOWARDS YOUR PROPOSED MIGRATION OR VISIT UNTIL YOUR APPLICATION HAS BEEN FINALIZED.**

IMPORTANT: Immigration medical results are only valid for 12 months from the date of the examination. If you have been notified that you will be required to attend a personal interview at a visa office, you should not/not schedule medical examination(s) until you have received your interview notice. **This will reduce the risk of expiry of medical results before completion of the processing of your application.**

1. It is possible that after the completion of your medical examination and submission of reports, further tests or reports may be requested.

2. It is recommended, and a decided advantage to all applicants, that routine immunizations for all children and adults be initiated or completed before departure for Canada, and where available, immunization records should be brought to Canada. This has many advantages for the applicant. For instance, a number of Canadian provinces require presentation of such records when children or adults enroll in school.

3. **To avoid unnecessary delays, please ensure that the physician:**

- answers all questions in Sections B through E of the Medical Report form;

- attaches original lab results;

- and forwards original chest x-ray(s) [DO NOT ROLL] to the address below:

Director, Health Programs (RNH)
Citizenship and Immigration Canada
Jean Edmond Towers South, 14th Floor
365 Laurier Avenue West
Ottawa, Ontario
K1A 1L1

4. If the Designated Medical Practitioner does not have Sections B to E, of the Medical Report Form (six pages) he/she may obtain them by writing to the address above.

MEDICAL EXAMINATION PROCEDURES

Persons applying for permanent residence to Canada must establish they are in good physical and mental health. Persons intending to remain in Canada as non-immigrants for more than six (6) months may also be required to undergo full examination. The cost of any medical examination must be borne by the person under examination.

Mental and Physical Examination

All applicants, regardless of age, are required to undergo a thorough medical examination by a physician, who will report the results on forms MS 1017. You may use only those physicians registered on the "Designated Medical Practitioners in the Greater Toronto Area" list. A single form MS 1017 is required for each person examined, including children of any age.

Important: Reports of Blood Wassermann and Urinalysis must be attached to MS 1017. Blood Serological Tests are not ordinarily required for children under fifteen (I5) years of age.

137

X-Ray and Radiological Examination

Must also be included as part of the examination. The x-rays may be taken through the physician conducting the medical examination or through hospitals or private laboratories. A radiologist's report and x-ray film must be submitted as part of the overall medical report; a complete medical assessment cannot be done unless both of the above are submitted. Applicants should, therefore, ensure that the x-ray film will be released to them or their physician in cases where the x-rays were taken in a hospital or laboratory. The x-ray film may be sent by the applicant or physician through the mail to the Immigrations medical authorities, address below. The above instructions apply to all applicants who have passed their eleventh (11th) birthday. A child under eleven years of age is required to submit an x-ray film of the chest and radiologist's report, if there is any indication of exposure to tuberculosis.

Passport Photographs

A standard unmounted passport photograph showing head and shoulders in a front view appropriate size 2" x 1-1/2" (5cm x 3-1/2cm) is to be submitted to the examining doctor for each member of the family undergoing a medical examination. Photographs are not required for infants under eighteen (18) months.

Further Procedures

Blood Wassermann, Urinalysis, Medical Reports and Passport Photographs respecting each member of the family will be submitted by the examining doctor preferably by Registered Mail to:

Citizenship & Immigration Canada,
International Service.
Health Program (OHP)
Ottawa, Ontario, K1A 0J9.
Attn: Deputy Director
Immigration Medical Assessment Unit.

Provisional Approval

When the results of the medical examination have been reviewed, the Immigration Medical Services will inform the Immigration Office dealing with application of the results. The Department of National Health and Welfare will not enter into correspondence with the person examined.

A medical Examination must be completed and forwarded to the above address prior to contacting this office for an interview.

How to Arrange your Medical Examination

To ensure prompt service, we encourage you to have a medical examination before you submit your application for permanent residence. It is your responsibility to arrange an appointment with a designated medical practitioner or through a private medical company in Canada, depending on where you live.

All applicants aged 11 and over must get a chest X-ray with a radiologist's report. This will be ordered by the designated examining physician. This is also required of children under age 11 if the child's medical history or the examination indicates a need or if there is evidence of tuberculosis in the family. The doctor will instruct you.

Immigration Medical Examination Already Completed

If you are applying for permanent residence as a live-in Caregiver and had an immigration medical examination before coming to Canada, and have not been out of the country for three consecutive months or mom, you may not require a further medical examination. You must send proof of the results of your medical examination (for example, a copy of your first employment authorization which should indicate medical results in the Remarks section) with your application.

Procedures

You may **not** use your own family doctor. If you do **not** follow the instructions below, you win be required to go to a Designated Doctor and will be required to pay the fees again.

Applicants in Ontario and Quebec

If you live in Toronto, Niagara Falls, Oakville, St. Catharines, Burlington, Oshawa or Hamilton or if your postal code begins with the letters J or H and you live in Montreal or the surrounding area, you must call one of the following numbers to arrange an appointment for your medical examination through a private medical company.

1-800-930-1232

If you are unable to reach any of these numbers, or if you live in Ontario or Quebec but outside the cities listed above, you may call one of the designated medical practitioners from the enclosed list.

Applicants in all provinces except Ontario and Quebec

Make an appointment with a doctor from the list of designated medical practitioners. The list is divided according to province. Choose the doctor most convenient for you.

All Applicants and their Dependents in Canada

When you go for your medical examination, take the following:

-- your passport;

-- your Immigration Client ID number (if you do not know the number or do not yet have a number, leave the space on the medical form blank);

-- eye glasses or contact lenses, if applicable;

-- any relevant medical reports;

-- four recent passport-size photographs, showing head and shoulders in a front view, approximately 50 mm X 70 mm;

-- form letter (**LET F**) in this kit which, when completed by the examining physician, will confirm that you have undergone a medical examination. Forward the completed letter to CPC Vegreville either with your application or later. (If you do not yet have an Immigration Client ID number or you do not know your number, leave the space on this form letter blank.)

Additional tests or reports, beyond the initial medical examination, may be required before a final medical assessment is rendered.

Applicants are responsible for all costs related to the medical examination.

CITIZENSHIP AND IMMIGRATION CANADA

Medical Examination – Frequently Asked Question

Will I receive a copy of the medical report and the result of the medical examination?

All medical reports and X-rays for the Immigration Medical Examination become the property of the Canadian Immigration Medical Authorities and cannot be returned to the applicant. The designated physician will not advise you of the results of the medical. The final decision on whether or not a medical is acceptable is determined by the visa office and not the designated physician. If your medical does not meet immigration requirements, the visa office will inform you by letter.

For how long is the medical examination valid?

The medical examination is valid for 12 months from the date of the first medical examination or test. If your visa is not processed in this time, you must take another complete examination.

Must everyone in my family have a medical examination?

Yes.

Can my own doctor do the medical examination?

No. The examination must be done by a doctor on Canada's list of *Designated Medical Physicians*.

My children are studying abroad and cannot return home for their immigration medical examination for another six months. I do not want to delay submitting my application. What should I do?

Whenever possible, all family members must be examined by the same designated physician. If this is impossible, arrange your medical with the designated physician and advise him/her that your dependants are abroad and will arrange to have their medical exams done by a designated physician closer to them. Then forward a copy of the *Medical Report Form* to each dependant with the addresses of their nearest designated physicians. This list of physicians may be obtained from the Visa Office. Ensure that the box titled "Name of Head of Family" in the *Medical Report Form* contains your name. Your dependants should then arrange to have their examinations. They should tell the designated physician to forward the completed medical report to the same Canadian medical office that received your report. Your dependant's medical will be matched with your file as the *Medical Report Form* will have your name written in the box titled "Name of Head of Family". NOTE: Medical instructions will normally be sent to you after you submit your application to the Visa Office.

I do not understand "excessive demand" or whether my ailment would place an excessive demand on Canada's health or social services. Can you tell me more?

The factors considered during the medical assessment include whether or not hospitalization or medical, social or institutional care are required and whether potential employability or productivity could be affected. For example, a person with a serious disease or psychiatric disorder that requires ongoing care or hospitalization may be inadmissible because their requirements would place "excessive demand" on the health-care system. Individuals with developmental delay or congenital disorders who require special education or training to lead an independent life may also be inadmissible. Other conditions which could place a significant financial burden on Canada's health or social services would also render an applicant medically inadmissible.

Can the doctor advise me regarding my application?

No. The doctor is only responsible for conducting a medical examination in accordance with Canada's immigration requirements. The designated physician cannot provide any advice on the immigration selection system.

CITIZENSHIP AND IMMIGRATION CANADA

Police Certificates

From USA

All applicants who are currently present in the USA or have stayed in the USA for six months or more must obtain Police Clearance from the **Federal Bureau of Investigation (FBI)**.

1. First, have your full set of fingerprints taken by a recognized agency.

· Fingerprints for US record checks should be taken on the FBI fingerprint form, but you should NOT CONTACT ANY FBI OFFICE FOR FINGERPRINTING. You may request a blank fingerprint form by writing to the FBI at the address below.

· In the USA, fingerprints can usually be obtained from a local police department. You <u>may</u> also be fingerprinted at a regional office of the Department of Motor Vehicles or from a private organization engaged in the fingerprinting business.
(Consult your local directory for such an establishment.) *Always specify that you require fingerprints for **Canadian** Immigration purposes.*

· When you appear for fingerprinting you will need **photo identification**, such as a passport, and a letter from the Canadian Consulate. Be prepared to provide fingerprinting agents with details of your full name (including maiden name) and any aliases, date of birth, sex, race, social security number, proof of your identity, and the reasons for requesting such a record, i.e. Canadian Visa purposes.

· Fees for fingerprinting differ depending on location.

2. Fingerprints should be sent, along with a certified cheque or money order for US$18 made payable to the U.S Treasury, to:

**FBI
Criminal Justice Information Services Division (CJIS Division)
1000 Custer Hollow Road
Clarksburg, West Virginia 26306
USA**

The processing of these requests normally takes between six (6) and eight (8) weeks.

3. The FBI will send you the results of their check by returning your fingerprint card to you. That will be your police certificate.

You should send the card and any attached documents to the Regional Program Centre. All police certificates must be ORIGINALS, photocopies will not be accepted by our office.

<u>UNITED STATES STATE POLICE CERTIFICATE REQUIREMENTS</u>

Alabama: State of Alabama, Department of Public Safety, Alabama Bureau of Investigation, Identification Unit, P.O. Box 1511, Montgomery, AL, 36192-1511 **Require:** 10 print Fingerprint form; Full Name, Race, Sex, Date of Birth and Social Security Number

Alaska: Department of Public Safety, Records & Identification Bureau, 5700 E Tudor Road, Anchorage, Alaska 99507. **Require:** Applicant's accurate address, reason for the request, Money order payable to the State of Alaska in the amount of US $35.00.

Arizona: Police certificates are not available.

Arkansas: Arkansas State Police, #3 Natural Resources Drive, Attention ID Bureau, P.O. Box

5901, Little Rock, Arkansas 72215 Tel: **(501) 221-8233 Require:** Name, Date of Birth, Place of Birth, Aliases, Sex, Names of towns, present and past addresses, Fee US $15.00, Money Order/Certified cheque

California: California Department of Justice, Applicant & Public Service Section, P.O. Box 903417, Sacramento, CA 94203-4170 Tel: **(916) 227-3822 Require:** Fingerprints, Money order payable to California Department of Justice in the amount of US $32.00.

Colorado: Colorado Bureau of Investigation, 690 Kipling Street, Suite 3000, Denver, CO 80215 Tel: **(303) 239-4300 Require:** Fingerprints; Money Order US $12.00.

Connecticut: Department of Public Safety, State Police Bureau of Identification, RO.Box2794, Middleton, CT. 06457-9294, Tel: **(860) 685-8480 Require:** Fingerprints & letter stating why certificate is necessary.

Delaware: Delaware State Police, P.O. Box 430, Dover, Delaware 19903 Tel **(302) 739-5900 Require:** Set of Fingerprints, Money Order/Certified Cheque US $25.00

District of Columbia: Metropolitan Police Department, Attn: Mail Correspondence, 300 Indiana Avenue NW, Suite 2100, Washington DC 20001 Tel: **(202) 727-4432 Require:** Self addressed envelope; Money Order/Certified cheque US $5.00 made out to the DC Treasury.

Florida: Florida Department of Law Enforcement, RO. Box 1489, Tallahassee, FL 32302 Attention: Criminal Records Inquiry Section. **Require:** Full name, Race, Sex, Date of Birth, Social Security Number

Georgia: Georgia Crime Information Centre, Attention: Special Handling Unit, RO. Box 370748, Decatur, GA 30037-0748 **Require:** 2 Finger print cards, full name, race, sex, date of birth, Social Security Number, US $7.50

Hawaii: State of Hawaii, Department of Attorney General, Hawaii Criminal Justice Data Centre, Attention: CHRC Unit, Room 101, 465 South King Street, Honolulu Hi 96813 **Require:** Name, aliases, Date of Birth, Social Security Number, Reason for request, sex, fingerprints. Money Order/Certified Cheque US $15.00.

Idaho: Department of Law Enforcement, Criminal Identification Bureau, P.O. Box 55, Boise, Idaho 83707

Illinois: Illinois State Police, Fee Processing Centre, 260 N. Chicago Street, Joliet, IL 60431 - 1075 **Require:** Certified Cheque/ Money Order US $14.00

Indiana: Indiana State Police - Record Division, 100 North Senate Avenue, Room 302, Indianapolis, IN 46204 Tel: **(317) 232-8262 Require:** Applicant must request for in writing, providing full name, date of birth, physical description and fingerprints.

Iowa: State-wide police certificates are not available. Applicants must apply to each local jurisdiction for local police certificates.

Kansas: Kansas Bureau of Investigation, Attention Records, 1620 SW Tyler Street, Topeka, Kansas 66612-1837 Tel: **(913) 296-8200 Require:** Return address in body of letter, reason for request, name, aliases, date of birth, place of birth and Social Security Number. Fee US $15.00

Kentucky: Department of State Police Records, 1250 Louisville Road, Frankfort, KY 40601, Tel: **(502) 227-8700 Require:** Full name, date of birth, social security number, past addresses in the State. Fee US $4.00 Money Order payable to State Treasury.

Louisiana: Louisiana State Police, Bureau of Identification, P.O. Box 66614, Baton Rouge, Louisiana 70896 Tel: **(504) 925-6095 Require:** Full names, date of birth, aliases, Social Security Number, reason for request. Fee US $10.00

Maine: Maine State Police, Bureau of Identification, 36 Hospital Street, Augusta, ME 04330

Maryland: CJIS Central Repository, P.O. Box 32708, Pikesville, MD 21208-2708, Pikesville, MD 21208 Tel: **(410) 764-4501 Require.** Fingerprints, US $18 Certified Cheque/Money Order payable to CJIS Central Repository

Massachusetts: Commissioner of Probations, 1 Ashburton Place, Room 401, Boston, MA 02108

Michigan: Michigan State Police, Central Records, General Office Building, 7150 Harris Drive, Lansing, MI 49813 Tel **(517) 322-5531 Require:** Fingerprints must be submitted on a standard fingerprint card on a standard fingerprint card available at local police stations. The RCMP fin- ger print form is not acceptable. US$15.OO Money Order payable to the State of Michigan.

Minnesota: Department of Public Safety, Bureau of Criminal Apprehension, 1246 University Avenue, St. Paul, MN 55104 Tel: **(612) 542-0672**

Mississippi: Police certificates are not available under state law. Records can only be provided to law enforcement agencies.

Missouri: Missouri State Highway Patrol, Crime Records Repository, 1510 E. Elm Street, Jefferson City, MO 651 01 **Require:** Fingerprints, Fee US $14.00

Montana: Montana Department of Justice, Identification Bureau, 303 Roberts, Helena, MT 59601 **Require:** Money Order/Certified Cheque US $5.00

Nebraska: Nebraska State Patrol, Criminal Investigation Division, Box 94637, State House Station, Lincoln NE 68509 **Require:** Application with money order/certified cheque US $10.00

Nevada: State police clearance letters are not available. Applicants who reside or have resided in Nevada obtain police clearance letters from the appropriate municipal police authorities.

New Hampshire: New Hampshire State Police, Criminal Records, 10 Hazen Drive, Concord, NH 03301

New Jersey: New Jersey Records and identification Section, Attn: Criminal information Units, Box 7068, West Trenton, NJ 08628-0068 **Require:** Fingerprints and a fee US $12.00

New Mexico: Department of Public Safety, P.O. Box 1268 or 4491 Cerrilos Street, Attention: Records Section, Santa Fe, NM 87504-1628 Tel: **(505) 827-9181**

New York State: New York State Division of Criminal Justice Services, Executive Park, Stuyvesant Plaza, Albany, NY 12203 Tel **(518) 457-6043 Require:** Applicants must submit a letter stating shy the check is required, the name, date of birth, sex, race, social security number, current address, previous addresses and a return address. Fingerprints required. Fee US $50.00

North Carolina: North Carolina State Bureau of Investigation, Division of Criminal Information, 407 North Blount Street, Raleigh, NC 27601 -1009 Attn: Stan Lewis **Require:** Full name, race, sex, date of birth, social security number and purpose of the request.

North Dakota: Bureau of Criminal Apprehension, Lock Box 1054, Bismark ND 58505

Ohio: State of Ohio, Office of Attorney General, Bureau of Criminal Identification and Investigation, P.O. Box 365, London, Ohio 43140 Tel: **(614) 852-2556 Require:** Full set of fingerprints; Waiver of release; Fee US $15.00

Oklahoma: Oklahoma State Bureau of Investigation, P.O. Box 11497, Attention: Criminal History Information, Oklahoma city, OK 73136 Telephone: **(405) 848-6724 Require:** US$ 10.00, Full name, aliases date of birth, social security number, sex and race and former addresss in the State.

Oregon: Dep't of State Police, Criminal Investigation Bureau, Public Service Building, 3772 Portland Rd, NE, Salem, Oregon 97310

Pennsylvania: Pennsylvania State Police, Records & Identification Division, 1800 Elmerton Avenue, Harrisburg, PA 17110 Tel **(717) 783-5592 Require:** Applicants must submit a "request for criminal check" form available through the Ohio State Police. Fee US $10.00 - Money Order or Certified cheque

Rhode Island: Chief Bureau of Criminal Investigation, Providence Superior Court House, 72 Pine Street, Providence, RI 02903

South Carolina: SLED Records, PO. Box 21398, Columbia, SC 29221 **Require:** Application must be made in writing providing name, race, sex, date of birth and social security number, Fee US $10.00

South Dakota: Division of Criminal Investigation, Criminal Justice Training Center, East Highway 34, c/o 500 East Capitol, Pierre SD 57501-5050

Tennessee: Police certificates are not available under state law. Records can only be provided to law enforcement agencies.

Texas: Department of Public Safety, Attention Crime Records Division, P.O. Box 15999, Austin, TX 78761-5999 Tel **(512) 465-2079 Require:** Applicants provide DPS fingerprint card, full name, social security number, date of birth, sex and drivers license number along with letter from applicant stating reason for requesting check. Addresses and towns in Texas in which the cient resided should also be provided. Fee: US $15.00 Money order/certified cheque.

Utah: State Bureau of Criminal Identification, Department of Public Safety, 4501 South 2700 Street West, Salt Lake City, Utah 84119. Tel: **(801) 965-4445 Require:** Fee US$ 10.00, Money order/certified cheque.

Vermont: Vermont Crime Information Centre, Department of Public Safety, P.O. Box 189, Waterbury, VT 05676

Virginia: Virginia State Police, Attention: Records Management Office, P.O. Box C-85076, Richmond VA 23261-5076, Tel: **(804) 674-2024**

Washington: Washington State Patrol, Identification Branch, P.O. Box 42633, Olympia, Washington 98504-2633, Tel **(206) 705-5100 Require:** Complete name (include maiden name) and date of birth. Fee: US $25.00, payable to Washington State Police.

West Virginia: West Virginia State Police, 725 Jefferson Road, South Charleston, W. VA 25309. **Require:** Application with Fee US $1 0.00.

Wisconsin: Wisconsin Department of Justice, Crime Information Bureau, attn: Record Check Unit, P.O. Box 2688, Madison, WI 53701-2688. **Require:** Application made by mail including name, date of birth, sex, and race of applicant. Fee: US $10.00.

Wyoming: State of Wyoming, Office of Attorney General, Division of Criminal Identification, Boyd Building, 4th floor, Cheyenne, WY 82002

Include your State Police Certificates and your FBI Results with your application for permanent residence

Police Certificates & Clearances

Security requirements

You and all your family members aged 18 and over who are not already Canadian citizens or permanent residents will be the subject of a background check, whether they will be accompanying you to Canada or not. To be admissible to Canada, you and your family members must not present any risk to Canada.

Background checks are intended to bar entry into Canada of those who may disrupt law and order, threaten the country's safety and security or be detrimental to national interests. Normally, Immigration authorities establish the admissibility of applicants for permanent residence and their family members through documents such as the immigration application form, police certificates and background records and assessments.

You must provide a police certificate for each country listed in table 1 and in which you have lived for more than six months since reaching 18 years of age. This document must indicate either any criminal record or the absence of a criminal record. It must be obtained for yourself, your spouse or common-law partner, and all of your family members aged 18 and over.

It is your responsibility to contact the police or relevant authorities in each of the jurisdictions concerned. Most countries have systems in place to obtain police certificates or clearances. The certificates are normally issued by police authorities, but in some countries you will have to apply to municipal, provincial, federal or similar governmental authorities for your record. Embassies or consulates of the countries concerned may be able to give you additional information.

You may have to provide information or documentation such as photographs, authorization to release personal information, fingerprints, or your addresses and periods of residence in other countries. Some authorities may require a letter from Canadian immigration authorities confirming that you have applied to immigrate to Canada and that you must obtain evidence of any criminal record as part of the processing of your application.

Criminality

Generally, persons with a criminal conviction are not admitted into Canada. However, if a prescribed period has passed after they have completed their sentence or committed an offence and during which they were not convicted of a subsequent offence, they may be deemed to have been rehabilitated. If they are not deemed to have been rehabilitated, they may, under special circumstances, be eligible to apply for rehabilitation.

Offences outside Canada

If you were convicted of or committed a criminal offence **outside** Canada, you may be deemed to have been rehabilitated if 10 years have passed since you have completed the sentence imposed upon you or since you have committed the offence, if the offence is one that would, in Canada, be an indictable offence punishable by a maximum term of imprisonment of less than 10 years. If the offence is one that would, in Canada, be prosecuted summarily and if you were convicted of two or more such offences, that period is 5 years after the sentence imposed was served or to be served.

Offences in Canada

If you have a criminal conviction **in** Canada, you must seek a pardon from the National Parole Board of Canada before you apply for immigration to Canada. For further information, contact:

Clemency and Pardons Division National Parole Board
410 Laurier Avenue West
Ottawa ON K1A 0R1
Telephone: 1-800-874-2652 (Callers in Canada and the United States only)
Facsimile: 1-613-941-4981
Web site: www.npb-cnlc.gc.ca (the guide which includes application forms can be downloaded

from the Web site)

If you have had two or more summary convictions in Canada, you may be deemed rehabilitated and no longer inadmissible if

• 5 years have passed since the sentence imposed was served or to be served,

• you have had no subsequent convictions and

• you have not been refused a pardon.

See Table 3 for a summary of the types of offences and length of rehabilitation periods.

If you or any of your family members have committed a criminal offence, you must provide, in addition to any police certificates or clearances, a full description of the circumstances surrounding the offence and the court record. This information will be reviewed by the visa office and you will receive further instructions.

We will also do our own background checks in all countries in which you and your family members have lived. These checks will determine if you have any arrests or criminal convictions, or if you are a security risk to Canada.

Table 1- Countries for which police certificates are required

Algeria	France	Luxembourg	Seychelles
Anguilla	French Guyana	Macao	Singapore
Antigua & Barbuda	French Polynesia	Malawi	South Africa
Australia	Gambia	Malaysia	Spain
Bahamas	Germany	Malta	Sri Lanka
Barbados	Ghana	Mauritius	Surinam
Belgium	Greece	Mayotte	Swaziland
Belize	Guyana	Montserrat	Sweden
Botswana	Honduras	Morocco	Switzerland
British Virgin Islands	Hong Kong	New Zealand	Syria
Brunei	Iceland	Namibia	Tanzania
Cayman Islands	Ireland, Republic of	Nigeria	Trinidad and Tobago
Costa Rica	Israel	Norway	Tunisia
Cyprus	Italy	Pakistan	Turkey
Denmark	Jamaica	Philippines	Turks & Caicos Islands
Dominica	Japan	Portugal	United States*
El Salvador	Jordan - West Bank only	St. Kitts & Nevis	Yugoslavia
Fiji		St. Lucia	Zambia
Finland	Kenya		Zimbabwe

*If you have lived in the United States, you must provide a state certificate AND a national

147

FBI certificate.

If you have lived in a country that is not on the above list, we may still do criminal checks on your behalf. We will contact you if we need more information.

If other countries where you have lived are added to this list, you will be asked to provide police certificates before your application is concluded.

Table 2 - Countries for which supplementary forms are required

If you have lived in one or more of the countries listed below, you **must** complete additional forms. If you do not already have them, contact a Call Centre for further information.

If other countries where you have lived are added to this list, you will be asked to provide police certificates before your application is concluded.

Argentina

Egypt

Germany

Israel

Japan

Republic of Ireland

South Korea

Sri Lanka

Switzerland

United States*

*Only if you have served in the U.S. military

We cannot process your application unless you have followed the additional instructions for the above countries.

If other countries where you have lived are added to this list, you will be asked to provide police certificates before your application is concluded.

Table 3 - Eligibility for Rehabilitation

Conviction or offence	Rehabilitation period	
	When deemed rehabilitated[1]	When eligible to apply for rehabilitation[3]
Indictable offence committed outside Canada, punishable by a maximum term of imprisonment of less than 10 years	10 years after completion of the sentence imposed	5 years after completion of the sentence imposed
Indictable offence committed outside Canada, punishable by a maximum term of imprisonment of less than 10 years	10 years after commission of the offence	5 years after commission of the offence
Two or more summary conviction offences committed in[2] or outside Canada	5 years after the sentence imposed is served or to be served	
Indictable offence committed in Canada	Must apply for a pardon	Must apply for a pardon

[1] The person must not have been convicted of a subsequent offence during the rehabilitation period.

[2] The person may be deemed rehabilitated only if a Canadian pardon has not been denied.

[3] The person must not have been convicted of a subsequent offence during the rehabilitation period.

CITIZENSHIP & IMMIGRATION CANADA

Frequently Asked Questions

<u>About the Application</u>?

What fees must I pay?

Your sponsor must pay a processing fee to support your application. The processing fee is non-refundable, even if your application is refused. The Right of Landing Fee (ROLF) is required of every adult aged 22 or over in your family but, unlike the processing fee, is refundable if an immigrant visa is not issued or used, or if you withdraw your application. The ROLF can be paid at any time during the application process, but must be paid before an immigrant visa can be issued. You will also have to pay other fees such as those related to the medical examination and police clearance.

Who is included in my application?

If you are married your spouse should be included as a dependent. You must also include on your application all dependent children whether they are accompanying you to Canada or not. (See "Important Words to Know" for a definition of dependent children.) Your dependents must pass background checks and medical examinations. All family members 18 years of age or over must complete their own individual application form.

What about my dependents who will not accompany me to Canada?

All of your dependents, whether they will accompany you to Canada or not, must pass medical examinations and background checks. All of your dependents, whether they will accompany you to Canada or not, must be included Part A of your application form or, if they are 18 or over, must complete their own application forms.

Should I pay someone to complete my forms and advise me on my application?

In some cases (for example, if you have difficulty understanding the form) you may wish to pay someone to help you fill in the information or to give you advice. However, this does not mean that your application will get special attention or necessarily be approved.

I cannot fit all the information on the application form and am unsure who should be included in my application.

You should complete the form by printing or typing clearly and you must sign your application form. If you need more space to answer any questions, attach separate pages. When you have signed the form, it becomes a legal document and the information you have provided must be truthful, complete and correct. It is an offence under the Immigration Act to knowingly make a false or misleading statement. If any information changes before you arrive in Canada (even if your visa has already been issued), you must inform the visa office to which you applied in writing.

Do I need a passport or travel document?

You and your dependents must have passports or travel documents which are valid. If any documents are soon to expire, you should renew them. Diplomatic, official, service or public affairs passports cannot be used to immigrate to Canada. You must have a valid regular or private passport when you arrive. The validity of your visa may be affected by the validity of your passport.

Must I or others in my family attend an interview?

A visa officer will review your application and decide if an interview is necessary. If so, you will be informed of the time and place. Your spouse and dependent children aged 18 or over will be

150

asked to come with you. The visa officer may ask about your job, work experience, education, reasons for migrating, plans and preparations. The officer may also ask about your family, spouse and/or dependents or your health, financial situation or past difficulties with the law. There may also be questions to determine your ability to settle successfully in Canada.

Do professionals need registration and licensing to work in Canada?

In Canada, approximately 20 percent of occupations are regulated to protect the health and safety of Canadians (e.g., nurses, engineers, teachers, electricians). People who want to work in regulated occupations need to obtain a license from a provincial regulatory body. Licensing requirements often include education from a recognized school, Canadian work experience and completion of a technical exam. Fees for exams can be costly and are the responsibility of the applicant. Final assessment by the provincial authority can only be done after you are in Canada with permanent resident status.

For how long is my immigrant visa valid?

Normally, immigrant visas are valid for 6-11 months from the date of issuance. The validity date is based upon the earlier of your or your dependents' passport validity date(s) or of the medical validity date. IMMIGRANT VISAS CANNOT BE EXTENDED ONCE ISSUED. IF APPLICANTS DO NOT USE THE VISAS WITHIN THEIR VALIDITY, THEY MUST REAPPLY FOR IMMIGRATION TO CANADA.

I intend to live in the Province of Quebec upon my arrival in Canada. Are there any special requirements for immigrating to this province?

Yes, if you wish to live in the Province of Quebec, your relative is required to obtain an undertaking with the Government of Quebec (referred to as an "engagement") assuming responsibility for you. Your sponsor will send you an original copy of this "engagement" which is to be attached to your application.

About the Medical Examination...

Will I receive a copy of the medical report and the result of the medical examination?

All medical reports and X-rays for the Immigration Medical Examination become the property of the Canadian Immigration Medical Authorities and cannot be returned to the applicant. The designated physician will not advise you of the results of the medical. The final decision on whether or not a medical is acceptable is determined by the visa office and not the designated physician. If your medical does not meet immigration requirements, the visa office will inform you by letter.

For how long is the medical examination valid?

The medical examination is valid for 12 months from the date of the first medical examination or test. If your visa is not processed in this time, you must take another complete examination.

Must everyone in my family have a medical examination?

Yes.

Can my own doctor do the medical examination?

No. The examination must be done by a doctor on Canada's list of Designated Medical Physicians.

My children are studying abroad and cannot return home for their immigration medical examination for another six months. I do not want to delay my application. What should I do?

Whenever possible, all family members must be examined by the same designated physician. If this is impossible, arrange your medical with the designated physician and advise him/her that your dependents are abroad and will arrange to have their medical exams done by a designated physician closer to them. Then forward a copy of the Medical Report Form to each dependent with the addresses of their nearest designated physicians. This list of physicians may be obtained from the Visa Office. Ensure that the box titled "Name of Head of Family" in the Medical Report Form contains your name. Your dependents should then arrange to have their examinations. They should tell the designated physician to forward the completed medical report to the same Canadian medical office that received your report. Your dependant's medical will be matched with your file as the Medical Report Form will have your name written in the box titled "Name of Head of Family". NOTE: Medical instructions will normally be sent to you after you submit your application to the Visa Office.

I do not understand "excessive demand" or whether my ailment would place an excessive demand on Canada's health or social services. Can you tell me more?

The factors considered during the medical assessment include whether or not hospitalization or medical, social or institutional care are required and whether potential employability or productivity could be affected. For example, a person with a serious disease or psychiatric disorder requiring ongoing care or hospitalization may be inadmissible because their requirements would place "excessive demand" on the health-care system. Individuals with developmental delay or congenital disorders who require special education or training to lead an independent life may also be inadmissible. Other conditions which could place a significant financial burden on Canada's health or social services would also render an applicant medically inadmissible.

Can the doctor advise me regarding my application?

No. The doctor is only responsible for conducting a medical examination in accordance with Canada's immigration requirements. The designated physician cannot provide any advice on the immigration selection system.

What happens if my application is refused?

If your application is refused, the visa office will inform you and your sponsor in writing. Your sponsor may appeal the decision to the Immigration and Refugee Board. It is important, therefore, that we always have your sponsor's latest address.

Upon Arrival ...

What happens when I arrive in Canada?

When you arrive, you must present your immigrant visa to a customs/immigration officer. The officer will check your visa and travel document and ask you questions similar to those on the immigration application form to verify that you are of good character and in good health. If there are no difficulties, the officer will authorize your admission to Canada as a permanent resident.

What settlement services are available?

Canada's settlement services are limited. You can learn about them from Canada Immigration Centres, Human Resources Development Centres and private organizations. Your sponsor and your sponsor's co-signer (if applicable) will have signed an undertaking with the Government of Canada to provide for your essential needs and those of your dependents for 10 years after you arrive in Canada to ensure that you do not become dependent on welfare. They must also sign a sponsorship agreement with you making the same commitment. In this agreement you, as the family class relative, agree to make every reasonable effort to provide for your own essential needs and those of your dependents.

Can you help me find a job?

Unfortunately we do not have the resources to provide this type of assistance.

After landing in Canada, what if I need to return to my country to settle my affairs?

Following landing in Canada, immigrants may leave and re--enter Canada if they spend less than six months in any 12-month period outside Canada. If immigrants are out of Canada for more than six months in any 12-month period, they will require a Returning Resident Permit to re--enter Canada. While such permits can be applied for either in Canada or overseas, they can only be applied for after the individual has been landed.

Your Rights and Obligations as a Permanent Resident of Canada

You and your dependents have the right to live, study and work for as long as you remain permanent residents in Canada, and are entitled to most social benefits accorded to Canadian citizens. When you have met citizenship requirements, you may apply for Canadian citizenship and a Canadian passport.

There are a few limitations on permanent residents:

-- You cannot vote in certain elections.

-- You may be ineligible for certain jobs requiring high-level security clearances.

-- As a permanent resident, you also have the same legal obligations as Canadians, such as paying taxes and respecting other laws.

-- If you or your dependents commit serious crimes, you or your dependents risk being deported from Canada.

Your sponsor and your sponsor's co-signer (if applicable) are **responsible for providing for your essential needs** and those of your dependents for 10 years after you arrive in Canada and for ensuring that you do not become dependent on welfare. Under the agreement you have signed with your sponsor and your sponsor's co-signer (if applicable), you are committed to making every reasonable effort to provide for your own essential needs and those of your dependents.

You remain a permanent resident until you become a Canadian citizen or abandon Canada as your place of residence. You may be considered to have abandoned Canada if you have frequent and/or lengthy absences from the country. If you travel to Canada to present your visas for landing and then return to live in your home country indefinitely, you will lose your permanent resident status.

IMPORTANT TELEPHONE NUMBERS

Immigration Law:

Immmigration Canada - Call Centre: **416-973-4444, 1-888-242-2100**

Immigration & Refugee Board: **416-954-1000**

USA Consulate: **416-595-1700**

USA Entry Waivers (if previously denied): **416-929-6011**

CITIZENSHIP AND IMMIGRATION CANADA

Interview Guidelines

WHO:

You, your spouse, all over-age eligible dependents who are included in your application must attend. Overage eligible dependents include single children aged 19 years or older, who have been attending school full-time since turning 19. Children under 19 years of age do not need to attend. If you show up for the interview without your wife or/and over-age dependents, the visa officer reserves the right to cancel the interview unless you have received prior approval by the visa office.

WHY:

The selection interview is aimed at assessing your ability to settle in Canada and to confirm the information you have provided so far. As a selection decision should be made during the interview, please make sure to bring all the supporting documentation needed according to your immigration category (see list attached). In all cases, you must produce a valid passport and a photocopy of a valid passport for each member of your family.

INTERPRETATION:

For those who cannot speak French or English with ease, the office will provide interpretation services in Arabic and Farsi. Applicants who are not familiar with any of these languages will have to make their own arrangements to come with a professional interpreter. The professional interpreter will have to produce documents of identification and proof of his/her professional status before the interview can begin. It must be mentioned that no immigration consultants will be allowed to assist their clients in interpretation. Please note that refugees who are referred by the UNHCR will be provided with interpretation services and do not need to make personal arrangements.

IF YOU CANNOT ATTEND ON THIS DATE:

In case you cannot attend this interview, be sure to inform the visa office at least two weeks in advance. Another appointment will be made on a priority basis. If you do not inform the visa office at least two weeks prior the interview, your file will be placed at the end of the interview queue. In all cases, only one more opportunity to attend the selection interview will be given. Failure to attend the second interview appointment will lead to the refusal of the application for non-compliance.

DOCUMENTS REQUESTED

PLEASE NOTE THAT ALL DOCUMENTS MUST BE TRANSLATED IN EITHER FRENCH OR ENGLISH BY A PROFESSIONAL TRANSLATOR. MAKE SURE TO BRING THE ORIGINAL DOCUMENTS.

FAMILY CLASS (PARENTS, CHILDREN, SPOUSES SPONSORED FROM CANADA)

- Birth certificate for applicant and dependents

- Marriage certificate

- Civil Marriage registration

- Divorce certificate for those who have been married previously

- Legal custody document for children whether accompanying or not

- Current school registration for dependents over 19 years of age (if applicable)

- Valid passport for each member of the family accompanying

- Military service card/Military service exemption card (if applicable)

- Police certificates issued within the last two months for applicant, spouse and children over 18 years of age

- Proof of relationship with sponsor in Canada

- Proof of residence and status of sponsor in Canada

IN ADDITION, FOR SPOUSES

- Proof of contacts with sponsor letters, phone bills, photos

FOR INDEPENDENT APPLICANTS (SKILLED WORKERS) AND ASSISTED RELATIVES

- Birth certificate for applicant, spouse and dependents

- Marriage certificate -Civil Marriage registration

- Divorce certificate for those who have been married previously

- Legal custody document for children whether accompanying or not

- Valid passport for each member of the family accompanying

- Military service card/Military service exemption card (if applicable)

- Police certificates issued within the last two months for applicant, spouse and children over 18 years of age

- Proof of relationship with a close relative living in Canada (if applicable)

- Proof of residence and status of a close relative living in Canada (if applicable)

- College certificates, diplomas and degrees for principal applicant and spouse

- Transcripts of courses for principal applicant and spouse

- Current school registration for dependents over 19 years of age and school transcripts and certificates for al years since the dependents turned 19 (if applicable)

- Letters of previous employers and current one for applicant and spouse.
- Updated bank statement and official value appraisal of properties

FOR BUSINESS APPLICANTS (ENTREPRENEURS, SELF-EMPLOYED, INVESTORS)

- Birth certificate for applicant, spouse and dependents

- Marriage certificate

- Civil Marriage registration

- Divorce certificate for those who have been married previously

- Legal custody document for children whether accompanying or not

- Valid passport for each member of the family accompanying

- Military service card/Military service exemption card (if applicable)

- Police certificates issued within the last two months for applicant, spouse and children over 18 years of age

- College certificates, diplomas and degrees for principal applicant and spouse

- Current school registration for dependents over 1 9 years of age and school transcripts and certificates for all years since the dependents turned 1 9. (if applicable)

- Letters of previous employers and current one for applicant and spouse

- Updated bank statement and official value appraisal of properties

- Official license, registration or incorporation documents for your company or shop

- Official audited financial reports for the last three years (if financial reports are not available, bring records books for the last three years)

- Business and personal taxation notification for the last three years

- Official authorization to export-import and trade (if applicable)

- Commercial and personal bank statements for the last three years

- Payrolls, list of employees, organizational charts

- Bills of lading

- Any other official documents that could support your experience and the funds available for immigration

- Photographs of the business owned and managed

FOR REFUGEES

- Any official documents confirming your identity

- UNHCR registration card

- Civil and professional documents that may be available

THE OFFICER MAY NOT NEED TO SEE ALL THE REQUIRED DOCUMENTS LISTED ABOVE IN EACH CASE. HOWEVER, ALL APPLICANTS MUST BRING THEM FOR THE INTERVIEW.

CITIZENSHIP AND IMMIGRATION CANADA

Where To Apply?

Part 1

Where to Apply for a Permanent Resident Visa

If you have been lawfully admitted for at least one year to one of the following countries, provinces or territories (or are a citizen of):	You must apply at the corresponding Canadian Visa Office in this column:
Afghanistan	Islamabad
Albania	Rome
Algeria	Paris
Andorra	Paris
Angola	Pretoria
Anguilla	Port of Spain
Anhui	Beijing
Antigua & Barbuda	Port of Spain
Argentina	Buenos Aires
Armenia	Moscow
Aruba	Caracas
Ascension	Accra
Ashmore and Cartier Island	Sydney
Australia	Sydney
Austria	Vienna
Azerbaijan	Ankara
B	
Bahamas	Kingston

Bahrain	London
Bangladesh	Singapore
Barbados	Port of Spain
Belarus	Warsaw
Belau, Republic of (or Palau)	Manila
Belgium	Paris
Belize	Guatemala City
Benin	Accra
Bermuda	Buffalo
Bhutan	New Delhi
Bolivia	Lima
Bonaire	Caracas
Bora Bora	Sydney
Boznia-Herzegovina	Vienna
Botswana	Pretoria
Brazil	Sao Paulo
British Indian Ocean Territory	Colombo
Brunei	Singapore
Bulgaria	Bucharest
Burkina-Faso	Abidjan
Burma (Myanmar, Union of)	Singapore
Burundi	Nairobi
C	

Cambodia	Singapore
Cameroon	Abidjan
Canada (for temporary lawful resident only)	Buffalo, or office responsible for your country of citizenship or, if stateless, your country of habitual residence (see this list).
Canary Islands	Paris
Cape Verde	Abidjan
Caroline Islands	Manila
Cayman Islands	Kingston
Central African Republic	Abidjan
Chad	Abidjan
Channel Islands	London
Chile	Santiago
China (see People's Republic of China)	
Choiseul	Sydney
Christmas Island	Sydney
Cocos (Keeling) Island	Sydney
Colombia	Bogota
Comoros Island	Nairobi
Cook Island	Sydney
Costa Rica	Guatemala City
Croatia	Vienna
Cuba	Havana
Curaçao	Caracas

Cyprus	Damascus
Czech Republic	Vienna
D	
Democratic Republic of the Congo	Abidjan
Denmark	London
Djibouti	Nairobi
Dominica	Port of Spain
Dominican Republic	Port-au-Prince
E	
East Timor	Singapore
Easter Island	Santiago
Ecuador	Bogota
Egypt	Cairo
El Salvador	Guatemala City
England	London
Equatorial Guinea	Abidjan
Eritrea	Nairobi
Estonia	Warsaw
Ethiopia	Nairobi
F	
Falkland Islands	Buenos Aires
Faroe Islands	London
Fiji	Sydney

Finland	London
France	Paris
French Guiana	Port-au-Prince
French Polynesia	Sydney
Fujian (PRC's province)	Hong Kong
G	
Gabon	Abidjan
Gambia	Accra
Gambier Island	Sydney
Gaza Strip (Palestinian Authority)	Tel Aviv
Georgia	Ankara
Germany	Berlin
Ghana	Accra
Gibraltar	Paris
Greece	Rome
Greenland	London
Grenada	Port of Spain
Guadalcanal	Sydney
Guadeloupe	Port-au-Prince
Guam	Manila
Guangdong (PRC's province)	Hong Kong
Guangxi (PRC's province)	Hong Kong
Guatemala	Guatemala City

Guinea (Refugees apply in Accra)	Abidjan
Guinea-Bissau	Abidjan
Guyana	Port of Spain
H	
Hainan (PRC's province)	Hong Kong
Haiti	Port-au-Prince
Honduras	Guatemala City
Hong Kong	Hong Kong
Huahine	Sydney
Hungary	Vienna
I	
Iceland	London
India	New Delhi
Indonesia	Singapore
Iran	Damascus
Iraq	Damascus
Ireland	London
Isle of Man	London
Israel	Tel Aviv
Italy	Rome
Ivory Coast	Abidjan
J	
Jamaica	Kingston

Japan	Manila
Jiangsu (PRC's province)	Beijing
Johnston Atoll	Manila
Jordan	Damascus
K	
Kazakhstan	Moscow
Kenya	Nairobi
Kiribati	Sydney
Kosrae (Micronesia)	Manila
Kuwait	London
Kyrgyzstan	Moscow
L	
Laos	Singapore
Latvia	Warsaw
Lebanon	Damascus
Lesotho	Pretoria
Liberia	Accra
Libya	Paris
Liechtenstein	Paris
Lithuania	Warsaw
Lord Howe Island	Sydney
Loyalty Island	Sydney
Luxembourg	Paris
M	

Macao	Hong Kong
Macedonia (Former Yugoslav Republic of)	Vienna
Madagascar (Republic of)	Nairobi
Maio	Sydney
Malawi	Pretoria
Malaysia	Singapore
Maldives	Colombo
Mali	Abidjan
Malta	Rome
Marianas	Manila
Marie-Galante	Port-au-Prince
Marquesas Island	Sydney
Marshall Island	Manila
Martinique	Port-au-Prince
Maupiti	Sydney
Mauritania	Abidjan
Mauritius	Nairobi
Mexico	Mexico City
Micronesia (Federated states of)	Manila
Midway Island	Manila
Moldova	Bucharest
Monaco	Paris
Mongolia	Beijing

Montserrat	Port of Spain
Moorea	Sydney
Morocco	Paris
Mozambique	Pretoria
Myanmar, Union of (Burma)	Singapore
N	
Namibia	Pretoria
Nauru	Sydney
Nepal	New Delhi
Netherlands	Berlin
Nevis	Port of Spain
New Caledonia	Sydney
New Georgia	Sydney
New Ireland	Sydney
New Zealand	Sydney
Nicaragua	Guatemala City
Niger	Abidjan
Nigeria	Accra
Niue Island	Sydney
Norfolk Island	Sydney
North Korea	Beijing
Northern Ireland	London
Northern Mariana Island	Manila

Norway	London
O	
Oman	London
P	
Pakistan	Islamabad
Palau (or Republic of Belau)	Manila
Palestinian Authority (West Bank & Gaza Strip)	Tel Aviv
Panama	Guatemala City
Papua New Guinea	Sydney
Paraguay	Buenos Aires
People's Republic of China* *Exception for Family Class applications only: office serving the provinces of: Fujian, Guangdong, Guangxi and Hainan is **Hong Kong**	Beijing or Hong Kong
Peru	Lima
Philippines	Manila
Pitcairn Island	Sydney
Pohnpei (Micronesia)	Manila
Poland	Warsaw
Portugal (Azores, Madeira)	Paris
Puerto Rico	Port of Spain
Q	
Qatar	London
R	
Raiatea	Sydney
Republic of Congo	Abidjan
Republic of Madagascar	Nairobi

Reunion	Nairobi
Romania	Bucharest
Russia	Moscow
Rwanda	Nairobi
S	
Saba	Port-au-Prince
Samoa (American & Western)	Sydney
San Marino	Rome
Santa Isabel	Sydney
Sao Tome and Principe	Accra
Saudi Arabia	London
Scotland	London
Senegal	Abidjan
Serbia-Montenegro	Vienna
Seychelles	Nairobi
Shanghai	Beijing
Sierra Leone	Accra
Singapore	Singapore
Slovakia	Vienna
Slovenia	Vienna
Society Archipelago	Sydney
Solomon Island	Sydney
Somalia	Nairobi
South Africa	Pretoria

South Korea	Seoul
Spain	Paris
Sri Lanka	Colombo
St Pierre et Miquelon	Buffalo
St. Barthelemay	Port-au-Prince
St. Eustatius	Port-au-Prince
St. Kitts	Port of Spain
St. Lucia	Port of Spain
St. Maarten/St. Martin	Port-au-Prince
St. Vincent and the Grenadines	Port of Spain
St. Helena	Accra
Sudan	Cairo
Suriname	Port of Spain
Svalbard	London
Swaziland	Pretoria
Sweden	London
Switzerland	Paris
Syria	Damascus
T	
Tahaa	Sydney
Tahiti	Sydney
Taiwan	Taipei
Tajikistan	Moscow

Tanzania	Nairobi
Thailand	Singapore
Togo	Accra
Tokeleau Island	Sydney
Tonga	Sydney
Tortola	Port of Spain
Trinidad & Tobago	Port of Spain
Tristan da Cunha	Accra
Truk Island (Micronesia)	Manila
Tuamotu Archipelago	Sydney
Tunisia	Paris
Turkey	Ankara
Turkmenistan	Ankara
Turks & Caicos	Kingston
Tuvalu	Sydney
U	
Uganda	Nairobi
Ukraine	Kyiv
United Arab Emirates	London
Uruguay	Buenos Aires
US Trust Territories of the Pacific Island	Manila
USA	Buffalo
Uzbekistan	Moscow
V	

Vanuatu	Sydney
Vatican City	Rome
Venezuela	Caracas
Vietnam	Singapore
Virgin Islands (British & US)	Port of Spain
W	
Wake Island	Manila
Wales	London
Wallis & Futuna	Sydney
West Bank (Palestinian Authority)	Tel Aviv
Western Sahara	Paris
Y	
Yap Island (Micronesia)	Manila
Yemen	London
Z	
Zambia	Pretoria
Zhejiang (PRC's province)	Beijing
Zimbabwe	Pretoria

Part 2

Where to Apply for a Temporary Resident Visa
(visitors, temporary workers and students)

To any of Canadian visa offices listed in **Part 1** of this annex, or to one of the Canadian missions listed below, as long as you have been lawfully admitted in the country in which you are present.

Important notice: if the office where you apply determines that an interview is required in order to make a decision on your application, you will have to attend such an interview at that office.

Africa and Middle East:

Abu Dhabi (United Arab Emirates)

Amman (Jordan)

Beirut (Lebanon)

Conakry (Guinea) (visitors and students only)

Dakar (Senegal) (visitors and students only)

Harare (Zimbabwe) (visitors and students only)

Kuwait City (visitors and students only)

Lagos (Nigeria)

Libreville (Gabon) (visitors and students only)

Lusaka (Zambia) (visitors and students only)

Rabat (Morocco)

Tunis (Tunisia)

Tehran (Iran)

Yaounde (Cameroon) (visitors and students only)

Asia and Pacific:

Shanghai (PRC) (only for visitors from provinces of Shanghai, Jiangsu, Anhui and Zhejiang)

Bangkok (Thailand)

Dhaka (Bangladesh)

Jakarta (Indonesia)

Kuala Lumpur (Malaysia)

Tokyo (Japan)

Europe:

Belgrade (Serbia-Montenegro)

Budapest (Hungary)

Prague (Czech Republic)

171

St-Petersburg (Russia)

Western Hemisphere:

Detroit (USA)

Los Angeles (USA)

New-York (USA)

Seattle (USA)

Washington (USA)

CITIZENSHIP AND IMMIGRATION CANADA

Things That May Delay Processing

- Incomplete or unsigned application forms

- Missing documents

- Incorrect or missing fees

- Insufficient postage

- Incorrect, incomplete address or failure to notify the visa office of a change of address

- Unclear photocopies of documents

- Documents not accompanied by a certified English or French translation

- You are not a permanent resident in the country in which you currently reside

- A medical condition that may require additional tests or consultations

- A criminal problem

- Family situations such as impending divorce or custody or maintenance issues

- Consultation is required with other offices in Canada and abroad

- Verification of information you give us

- inquiring about the status of your application before the standard processing time has passed.

It is an offence under the *Immigration Act* to knowingly make a false or misleading statement in connection with an application for permanent residence in Canada.

Enforcement

Canada has a generous immigration policy which includes reasonably-open borders and an equitable system of justice and appeals. However, some people, such as document forgers and other criminals, attempt to avoid this immigration process. For the protection of society and to uphold the established legislation, people who enter or attempt to enter Canada using false or misleading information are not wanted in the country. Stopping illegal migrants and undesirables overseas at ports of entry before they arrive in Canada is the first step in this process.

INADMISSIBILITY

Who is admissible?

Canadian citizens and persons registered as Indians pursuant to the *Indian Act* have the right to enter or remain in Canada. Permanent residents can enter the country and remain unless they have given up or lost their permanent resident status or have taken part in activities that make them subject to removal. Other persons wanting to come to Canada as immigrants and visitors may be granted admission if they possess a valid visa (if required), pose no risk to Canada, and are not inadmissible for some other reason.

Who is inadmissible?

Persons may be denied a visa, refused admission, or removed from Canada if, for example:

· the immigration officer believes them to be non-genuine visitors (persons whose real intent is to remain indefinitely);

· two Medical Officers believe that they are likely to be a danger to public health or to cause excessive demands on health or social services;

· they are unable or unwilling to support themselves and their dependants;

· they have been convicted of criminal offences or reasonable grounds exist to believe that they have committed a crime;

· they have engaged in acts of espionage, subversion or terrorism, or reasonable grounds exist to believe that they will engage in such activities;

· they are, or were, members of criminal, violent, terrorist or subversive organizations, or

· reasonable grounds exist to believe that they will take part in acts of violence, subversion or terrorism while in Canada;

· they constitute a danger to the security of Canada;

· there are reasonable grounds to believe that they have committed a war crime or crime against humanity;

· they are, or were, senior members or senior officials in the service of a government that is or was engaged in terrorism, systematic or gross human rights violations, war crimes or crimes against humanity;

· they have remained in Canada longer than authorized;

· they have previously been deported and are seeking to enter Canada without the consent of the Minister;

· they have taken a job or attended an educational institution without authorization; or

175

· they have violated any terms or conditions of their admission or have violated other provisions of the *Immigration Act* or *Regulations.*

Depending on the circumstances, prospective visitors who are found to be inadmissible for minor offences may be granted discretionary entry for up to 30 days (non-extendible). Appropriate terms and conditions may be imposed in these cases and a processing fee will be collected. (Refer to the Fee Schedule, for details on processing fees.)

BACKGROUND CHECKS

A background check is a normal part of immigrant visa processing. The procedure is intended to bar the entry into Canada of those who may disrupt law and order, threaten the country's security, or otherwise be detrimental to national interests.

Background checks are done for everyone aged 18 to 65 before they receive an immigrant visa. Documents used in these checks include:

· the immigration application form;

· security, intelligence and criminal conviction records; and

· immigration records for persons who have violated provisions of the *Immigration Act.*

Background checks may also be done before a visa is issued to a visitor if there is reason to believe that the visitor may be undesirable or prohibited by immigration law. In some countries, a waiting period is required for background checks.

RESPONSIBILITIES OF TRANSPORTATION COMPANIES

According to the *Immigration Act* and *Regulations,* transportation companies must ensure that passengers are presented for examination at ports of entry with valid travel documents and visas if required. Canadian officials provide airlines with training and technology to help identify improperly documented passengers before they embark for Canada. If passengers are improperly documented and are allowed passage to Canada, the company may be charged an administration fee of $3,200 to help pay the cost of processing the inadmissible person.

As a general rule, transportation companies are required to pay the costs of return transportation and medical costs of passengers refused admission to Canada, but are not required to pay the removal costs if passengers arrive with a valid visa.

Citizenship and Immigration Canada also requires security deposits from carriers to cover liabilities incurred under the *Act.* If the carrier refuses, the vehicle can be detained for up to 48 hours or seized and sold to recover monies owed.

Transportation companies also have responsibilities related to crew members. These include the presentation of crew lists and the reporting of crew changes and deserters. Carriers must also report stowaways and guard them safely before transferring them into the custody of an immigration officer.

CONTROL AT THE BORDER

Canadian control initiatives have resulted in declining numbers of improperly documented passengers arriving in Canada. However, "people smuggling" is an ongoing concern. Immigration officers have the authority to search travellers when documentation relating to identity and nationality is missing or inadequate. Travel documents may also be held by immigration officials to ensure that they are available for possible removal action taken under the *Immigration Act.*

OTHER ENFORCEMENT MEASURES

Other measures may also be taken against those who abuse or take advantage of Canada's immigration laws. They include:

· Increased penalties for smuggling migrants. The penalties now range from fines of $10,000 to $500,000, imprisonment for up to 10 years, or both.

· Stronger measures against those who make multiple refugee claims. Although the number of people involved in duplicate refugee claims is small, the problem is serious. Once duplicate refugee claims are processed, multiple applications for welfare can also be made. Fingerprinting and photographing of refugee claimants is carried out to deal with this problem. Fingerprinting can also help to detect criminals attempting to enter Canada as refugees. Fingerprints of successful refugee applicants are destroyed once they receive Canadian citizenship.

· Preventing social assistance abuse by visitors. Visitors to Canada who would cause or be reasonably expected to cause excessive demand on health or social services can be removed.

CITIZENSHIP AND IMMIGRATION CANADA

Your Rights & Obligations As A Permanent Resident

You and your dependants have **the right to live, study and work** for as long as you remain permanent residents in Canada, and are entitled to most social benefits accorded to Canadian citizens. When you have met citizenship requirements, you may apply for Canadian citizenship and a Canadian passport.

There are a **few limitations** on permanent residents:

· You **cannot vote** in certain elections.

· You may be ineligible for certain jobs requiring high-level security clearances.

· As a permanent resident, you also have **the same legal obligations** as Canadians, such as paying taxes and respecting other laws.

· If you or your dependants commit **serious crimes**, you or your dependants risk being deported from Canada.

You remain a permanent resident until you become a **Canadian citizen** or abandon Canada as your place of residence. You may be considered to have abandoned Canada if you have frequent and/or lengthy absences from the country. If you travel to Canada to present your visas for landing and then return to live in your home country indefinitely, you will lose your permanent resident status.

CITIZENSHIP AND IMMIGRATION CANADA

Printed in the United States
118195LV00003B/20/A